The Cocker Spaniel

Our Best Friends

OUR BEST FRIENDS

The Cocker Spaniel

Karen Schweitzer

ELDORADO INK

Produced by OTTN Publishing, Stockton, New Jersey

Eldorado Ink
PO Box 100097
Pittsburgh, PA 15233
www.eldoradoink.com

CPSIA compliance information: Batch#OBF010111-4. For further information,
contact Eldorado Ink at info@eldoradoink.com.

First printing

1 3 5 7 9 8 6 4 2

Library of Congress Cataloging-in-Publication Data

Schweitzer, Karen.
  The cocker spaniel / Karen Schweitzer.
     p. cm. — (Our best friends)
  Includes bibliographical references and index.
  ISBN 978-1-932904-76-5 (hardcover) — ISBN 978-1-932904-82-6 (trade)
  1. Cocker spaniels—Juvenile literature. I. Title.
  SF429.C55S39 2011
  636.752'4—dc22

                    2010034486

Photo credits: © American Animal Hospital Association, 74; © Greg Nicholas/iStock
photo.com: 63; © Jupiter Images: 41, 53; Library of Congress: 20; used under license from
Shutterstock, Inc., 3, 8, 10, 11, 12, 15, 16, 17, 18, 21, 23, 24, 25, 26, 28, 30, 31, 32, 34,
35, 38, 42, 43, 44, 45, 47, 48, 50, 51, 52, 55, 56, 60, 61, 62, 63, 65, 66, 68, 70, 73, 78, 81,
84, 88, 89, 90, 93, 94, 96, 98, 100, front cover (all), back cover.

**For information about custom editions, special sales, or premiums,
please contact our special sales department at info@eldoradoink.com.**

TABLE OF CONTENTS

Introduction

The mutually beneficial relationship between humans and animals began long before the dawn of recorded history. Archaeologists believe that humans began to capture and tame wild goats, sheep, and pigs more than 9,000 years ago. These animals were then bred for specific purposes, such as providing humans with a reliable source of food or providing furs and hides that could be used for clothing or the construction of dwellings.

Other animals had been sought for companionship and assistance even earlier. The dog, believed to be the first animal domesticated, began living and working with Stone Age humans in Europe more than 14,000 years ago. Some archaeologists believe that wild dogs and humans were drawn together because both hunted the same prey. By taming and training dogs, humans became more effective hunters. Dogs, meanwhile, enjoyed the social contact with humans and benefited from greater access to food and warm shelter. Dogs soon became beloved pets as well as trusted workers. This can be seen from the many artifacts depicting dogs that have been found at ancient sites in Asia, Europe, North America, and the Middle East.

The earliest domestic cats appeared in the Middle East about 5,000 years ago. Small wild cats were probably first attracted to human settlements because plenty of rodents could be found wherever harvested grain was stored. Cats played a useful role in hunting and killing these pests, and it is likely that grateful humans rewarded them for this assistance. Over time, these small cats gave up some of their aggressive wild behaviors and began living among humans. Cats eventually became so popular in ancient Egypt that they were believed to possess magical powers. Cat statues were placed outside homes to ward off evil spirits, and mummified cats were included in royal tombs to accompany their owners into the afterlife.

Today, few people believe that cats have supernatural powers, but most pet owners feel a magical bond with their pets, whether they are dogs, cats, hamsters, rabbits, horses, or parrots. The lives of pets and their people become inextricably intertwined, providing strong emotional and physical rewards for both humans and animals. People of all ages can benefit from the loving companionship of a pet. Not surprisingly, then, pet ownership is widespread. Recent statistics indicate that about 60 percent of all households in the United States and Canada have at least one pet, while the figure is close to 50 percent of households in the United Kingdom. For millions of people, therefore, pets truly have become their "best friends."

Finding the best animal friend can be a challenge, however. Not only are there many types of domesticated pets, but each has specific needs, characteristics, and personality traits. Even within a category of pets, such as dogs, different breeds will flourish in different surroundings and with different treatment. For example, a German Shepherd may not be the right pet for a person living in a cramped urban apartment; that person might be better off caring for a smaller dog like a Toy Poodle or Shih Tzu, or perhaps a cat. On the other hand, an active person who loves the outdoors may prefer the companionship of a Labrador Retriever to that of a small dog or a passive indoor pet like a goldfish or hamster.

The joys of pet ownership come with certain responsibilities. Bringing a pet into your home and your neighborhood obligates you to care for and train the pet properly. For example, a dog must be housebroken, taught to obey your commands, and trained to behave appropriately when he encounters other people or animals. Owners must also be mindful of their pet's particular nutritional and medical needs.

The purpose of the OUR BEST FRIENDS series is to provide a helpful and comprehensive introduction to pet ownership. Each book contains the basic information a prospective pet owner needs in order to choose the right pet for his or her situation and to care for that pet throughout the pet's lifetime. Training, socialization, proper nutrition, potential medical issues, and the legal responsibilities of pet ownership are thoroughly explained and discussed, and an abundance of expert tips and suggestions are offered. Whether it is a hamster, corn snake, guinea pig, or Labrador Retriever, the books in the OUR BEST FRIENDS series provide everything the reader needs to know about how to have a happy, well-adjusted, and well-behaved pet.

The handsome, energetic, and intelligent Cocker Spaniel has been among the most popular dog breeds over the past century. Whether you want a show dog or are just looking for a family pet, a Cocker Spaniel might be the right dog for you.

CHAPTER ONE

Is a Cocker Spaniel Right for You?

The Cocker Spaniel's high intelligence, merry personality, and soft, melting eyes have made this purebred dog one of the most popular breeds in the United States and elsewhere in the world. They are the smallest members of the sporting dog family, but they have big hearts that can make a dog lover out of almost anyone.

Cocker Spaniels are affectionate, loyal, and enjoy spending time with their owners. Most Cocker Spaniels are also very active and willing to participate in almost any activity. Dogs of this breed are natural hunters and take to the water well, whether it's a lake or a swimming pool. Anyone who has ever seen a Cocker Spaniel in the show ring knows why this little dog is considered a magnificent competitor.

If you have been thinking about purchasing a Cocker Spaniel, there are a few things you should know before being captivated by the breed's cuteness. Cocker Spaniels aren't for everyone. They have an intense love of play and need daily walks and exercise periods to burn off energy. Cocker Spaniels can also be very noisy when they are excited, upset, or in the mood to express themselves.

Another consideration for would-be-owners of this breed is grooming. Cocker Spaniels have long, luxurious coats that require daily attention. Grooming can be greatly reduced if the dog is given a shorter haircut,

Affectionate Cocker Spaniels often make good pets for families with children.

known as a pet trim or utility clip. But even short hair needs weekly brushing and a fair amount of bathing and trimming.

PHYSICAL CHARACTERISTICS

Many people consider the Cocker Spaniel to be an ideal size. Dogs of this breed are small enough to sit in a lap or to be carried for short distances, but they are also sturdy enough to romp with children or run through a forest if that's what the occasion requires. Some of the other physical characteristics that make Cocker Spaniels stand out from other breeds include long ears, a docked tail, soulful eyes, and a beautiful feathered coat.

Buff is the traditional color for Cocker Spaniels and the one most associated with the breed. The color black is also relatively common. Other solid colors often seen on Cocker Spaniels include brown, red, and silver. The AKC categorizes these colors as ASCOB (Any Solid Color Other Than Black.)

A Cocker Spaniel's coat can also include a combination of colors. Dogs of this variety are known as parti-colored dogs. They are not as common as their monochromatic counterparts, but are just as pleasing to the eye. Parti-color Cocker Spaniels may have two or more solid colors, one of which is usually white.

Other unusual color combinations include merle and roan. Both are very rare. Merle-patterned dogs have a special gene that dilutes the color of some of the hairs in their coat. This dilution can give the hair a very unique appearance, and may even make black hair take on a brilliant bluish sheen. Roan-patterned dogs have a predominant color that develops progressively throughout their coat. These dogs may also appear blue if the coat is peppered heavily enough with the predominant color.

AMERICAN VERSUS ENGLISH COCKER SPANIELS

The term *Cocker Spaniel* is often used to describe two separate breeds of dog: the American Cocker Spaniel and the English Cocker Spaniel. Both are generally known as simply the "Cocker Spaniel" in their countries of origin.

The American Kennel Club first acknowledged the English Cocker Spaniel as a breed of dog separate from the American Cocker Spaniel in 1946. Although the two breeds share the same history and many of the same characteristics, slight physical

Cocker Spaniels are active, athletic dogs that enjoy playing with their owners.

FAST FACT

Cocker Spaniels get along well with many animals, including cats and other breeds of dogs.

differences do exist. English Cocker Spaniels are larger than their American counterparts. They also tend to have a narrower head and chest and a longer back.

Despite the physical differences, both types of Cocker Spaniels have many of the same needs when it comes to training and care. It is safe to assume that any advice in this book can pertain to both breeds unless otherwise noted.

A COCKER SPANIEL'S ROLE IN YOUR LIFE

Cocker Spaniels are a versatile breed and adapt well to most situations. This flexibility allows them to play many different roles in the lives of their owners. One of the most common roles for Cocker Spaniels is that of companion. The breed's happy disposition, intelligence, and small size make them ideal housedogs. Cocker Spaniels are also known for being very family-oriented, which makes them a good choice for homes with young children.

Cocker Spaniels make great hunting companions as well. Over the years, these dogs have maintained their natural ability to hunt, track, and flush out game. Cocker Spaniels make good gun dogs and are more than willing to spend a day in the field or in the woods with their owners. The breed also excels in conformation, tracking, and agility competitions. Training Cocker Spaniels to hunt or participate in competitive events can take some time, but can be very rewarding for both of you.

Cocker Spaniels have sensitive noses that can sniff out the faintest scents. These dogs can even follow a trail that is weeks old.

THE BEST ENVIRONMENT FOR A COCKER SPANIEL

The best environment for a Cocker Spaniel is one that provides regular attention. Dogs of this breed are social creatures and crave companionship. If they are left alone for too long, they will pine for their owners and may even become destructive.

Cocker Spaniels are also very athletic and need moderate exercise. Although they do well in apartments and compact homes, they do require daily walks and room to run on

DOCKED VS. UNDOCKED TAILS

According to the American Kennel Club's breed standards, descriptions of the ideal characteristics for both American and English Cocker Spaniels, these dogs' tails should be docked, or amputated. This is an old tradition that is still alive today, although it is not without controversy.

Historically, the tails of hunting dogs like Cocker Spaniels were docked for practical purposes. A dog's wagging tail can become tangled in brush or bang against something and become injured. Damage to the tail does not heal easily; it can become infected and may eventually affect a dog's overall health. Even though Cocker Spaniels today are more likely to be pets and show dogs, the practice of docking persists.

Tail docking is painful for the dog, so today some American breeders opt not to perform this procedure on their puppies. Germany and several other European countries have outlawed tail docking. The breed standards adopted by the Kennel

Club of the United Kingdom for both English and American Cocker Spaniels allow for tails to be either docked or undocked. In the United States, an undocked tail is not explicitly listed as a disqualifying fault for a dog competing in an AKC-sanctioned conformation event. However, many experts would agree that undocked Cocker Spaniels are not likely to win such events.

Chances are that you'll have no say in the matter of whether your dog's tail is docked or undocked. Cocker Spaniel puppies usually have their tails docked a few days after they are born. This is because nerves in the tail have not yet fully developed, so the amount of pain the puppy feels is limited. If your Cocker Spaniel has not had his tail docked when you pick him up, he should probably be left undocked. In addition to greater pain, other serious complications, such as bleeding and infection, can result from the surgery when done on an older puppy or dog.

FAST FACT

The American Kennel Club combines breeds with similar characteristics into groups. Cocker Spaniels are in the sporting group. Some other breeds in the sporting group include the Field Spaniel, Irish Setter, Labrador Retriever, and Golden Retriever.

occasion. A fenced-in backyard is ideal, as it will allow your Cocker Spaniel to safely stretch his legs.

Of course, you should not leave your pet in the backyard unsuper-

vised for long periods. Cocker Spaniels are very curious and intelligent. If a Cocker Spaniel sees something outside the yard that he wants, or gets bored from lack of company, there is a good chance he'll find a way through the fence.

BASIC COSTS OF DOG OWNERSHIP

Owning a dog isn't cheap. In addition to the purchase price, there are veterinary costs and assorted day-to-day expenses. It is not unusual for a Cocker Spaniel owner to spend hundreds, and possibly thousands, of dollars each year on basic expenses. Knowing what sorts of

THE AMERICAN KENNEL CLUB

The American Kennel Club (AKC) is a nonprofit organization that maintains a purebred dog registry. The group, founded in 1884, tracks data and statistics for 157 dog breeds. The AKC records puppy births, registrations for individual dogs, and titles earned in dog shows and other events.

In addition to maintaining a registry, the AKC sponsors a variety of events that are held by member clubs, such as the American Spaniel Club and the English Cocker Spaniel Club of America. These

events include dog shows, agility trials, tracking tests, and obedience competitions. The AKC sanctions and promotes events to uphold standards and garner interest from spectators.

Other AKC objectives include advancing the study of purebred dogs and promoting the health and well-being of all dogs. The AKC prides itself on being an advocate for dog owners and responsible dog ownership. You can learn more about the AKC by visiting the club online at www.akc.org.

Prospective owners must be prepared to make a long-term commitment before acquiring a Cocker Spaniel. The average Cocker Spaniel can live to be 14 or 15 years old.

costs are involved before purchasing a dog is an absolute must. Some of the basic costs associated with responsible Cocker Spaniel ownership include:

ROUTINE VETERINARY CARE: Every Cocker Spaniel needs an initial veterinary exam as well as yearly wellness exams. Healthy senior dogs (age seven and above) should be examined every six months. The cost of this can vary depending on the vet and the thoroughness of the exam. Cocker Spaniel owners can expect to

pay anywhere between $20 and $200 for each examination.

PARASITE TESTS AND PREVENTION: Heartworms, roundworms, and other internal parasites can make a Cocker Spaniel very ill and may even cause death in extreme cases. Puppies need to be tested for parasites when they receive their first veterinary exam. After that, Cocker Spaniels should be tested annually. If worms are present, the veterinarian will provide medication to kill the parasites. If not, the vet will supply preventive

FAST FACT

The entertainment world's most famous Cocker Spaniel is Lady from the Walt Disney animated movie *Lady and the Tramp*. The movie, first released in 1955, prompted thousands of U.S. children to beg their parents for a Cocker Spaniel.

medication. Typically, the costs of lab testing and medication range between $100 and $150 each year for healthy dogs.

IMMUNIZATIONS: Every Cocker Spaniel puppy requires a series of inoculations to protect against distemper, hepatitis, leptospirosis, parainfluenza, and parvovirus. At about six months old, puppies need a rabies shot. After receiving initial inoculations, adult dogs need regular booster shots to protect against these diseases. Other immunizations a Cocker Spaniel may need include vaccinations for Lyme disease, kennel cough, and coronavirus. The cost for immunizations varies, but owners can expect to spend between $20 and $150 each year.

SPAYING OR NEUTERING: Cocker Spaniels that will not be bred or entered into formal competitions should be spayed or neutered as soon as possible. This will prevent unwanted pregnancies and may reduce the likelihood of life-threatening illnesses, such as cancer and pyometra (an infected uterus). Spaying or neutering is a onetime cost that usually ranges from $50 to $300.

GROOMING SUPPLIES: Compared to some breeds, Cocker Spaniels need a great deal of grooming. They should be brushed daily, and require regular baths and coat trims. Professional grooming can become very expensive. Groomers usually charge between $30 and $150 per session, and a Cocker Spaniel will require at least one session a month to look his best. Grooming a Cocker Spaniel at home is less expensive but more time

Cocker Spaniel puppies love to chew things. Provide your pup with nylon bones or sturdy chew toys to keep him occupied.

consuming. Necessary supplies for Cocker Spaniel grooming include a brush, shampoo, nail clippers, and a special shower nozzle. The cost for these items is minimal.

FLEA AND TICK PREVENTION: Fleas can drive a Cocker Spaniel mad. Their bites cause severe itching and discomfort. Flea bites can also create serious health problems and may result in hair loss, skin infections, anemia, and allergic reactions. Ticks can cause similar problems, and they may carry Lyme disease as well. A Cocker Spaniel owner can expect to spend between $50 and $150 on flea and tick prevention each year. Prevention, it must be noted, is much cheaper than treatment.

FOOD: Cocker Spaniels love food and will eat as much as they can get. An adult Cocker Spaniel can be expected to eat between 365 and 730 cups of dry food per year. The

Cocker Spaniels thrive on love and attention from their owners.

cost of food varies greatly, depending on the brand and the ingredients. The higher the quality, the higher the price. It is not unreasonable for a Cocker Spaniel owner to spend more than $500 each year on dog food.

MISCELLANEOUS COSTS: Caring for a Cocker Spaniel requires other supplies as well. These include, but are not limited to: a crate, bedding, a collar, a leash, dog bowls, toys, treats, dog tags, and training supplies. There is really no limit to what you can buy or how much you can spend on your canine companion.

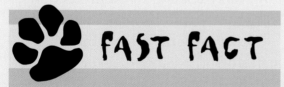

FAST FACT

If you work full-time or spend long hours away from home each day, you could put your pet in doggie day care or hire a pet sitter so that he will have some companionship during that time.

CHAPTER TWO

Cocker Spaniel History and Breed Standard

Like all spaniels, the Cocker Spaniel breed probably originated in the country of Spain. Before the invention of firearms, hunters used spaniels to help them chase or flush out small game, like rabbits, pheasant, and woodcock. The spaniel's body was compact but strong enough to push through dense shrubbery and navigate tangled thickets in search of game. Their long, silky coats offered protection from thorns and brambles.

Breed experts believe that the ancestors of today's Cocker Spaniel may have been brought to England more than 600 years ago. The first mention of a "spanyell" dog occurs in

A black American Cocker Spaniel fetches a stick from the water. Dogs of the Cocker Spaniel breed were originally prized for their ability to hunt in ponds and marshes.

an English manuscript from the 14th century. These dogs soon became popular among wealthy British hunters who had heard tales of the breed's hunting prowess.

Cocker Spaniels did not begin to be considered a dog breed separate from other types of spaniels until the 19th century. At that time, spaniel dogs began to become differentiated by their size and inherent hunting ability. Spaniels that had a talent for "springing," or flushing birds from cover, were called Springing Spaniels. Dogs that were adept at hunting woodcocks, a type of wading bird commonly found in shallow, reedy ponds, became known as Cocking Spaniels.

In the mid-1870s, British dog fanciers created the first breed standards for spaniels. A breed standard, sometimes called a standard of perfection, is a description of the ideal characteristics possessed by a purebred dog of a certain breed. In 1885, a club called the Spaniel Club was formed in Britain to oversee the breeding and standards for the purebred dogs of this type.

In 1892, the Spaniel Club officially introduced the names Springer Spaniel and Cocker Spaniel to identify spaniels with different characteristics. Other types of spaniels were identified as well, such as the Field Spaniel, Norfolk Spaniel, and English Water Spaniel.

THE COCKER SPANIEL IN AMERICA

In 1892, the Kennel Club of the United Kingdom officially recognized the Cocker Spaniel as a separate breed of dog. Many Cocker Spaniel owners were pleased with this turn of events. However, it wasn't long before a new debate emerged among fanciers of the breed. The disagreement involved two distinct types of Cocker Spaniels that were beginning to take shape at the turn of the 20th century—one in the United Kingdom, and the other in the United States.

Spaniels have a long history in North America. The first spaniel in America arrived on the Mayflower in 1620, and was used to hunt game in the original Plymouth colony of New England. Over the next few centuries, spaniels became popular dogs in America. The American Kennel Club registered its first purebred

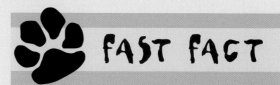

FAST FACT

The American Spaniel Club was the first breed club established in the United States.

By the early 20th century, Cocker Spaniels had become popular among wealthy dog fanciers, such as socialite and activist Florence "Daisy" Harriman, pictured with her Cocker Spaniel Bart in 1937.

er coats. They also had smaller heads and muzzles.

By 1935, the two types of Cocker Spaniels, English and American, were different enough that separate categories were created for judging each type in dog shows. In 1938, the English Cocker Spaniel Club of America decided to make a clear distinction between the American Cocker Spaniel and the English Cocker Spaniel. This prevented interbreeding and allowed the English fanciers to preserve the appearance of the original English Cocker Spaniels, while the American breeders could go their own way.

In September 1946, the American Kennel Club granted separate breed status to the American Cocker Spaniel and the English Cocker Spaniel. Approximately 20 years later, the Kennel Club of the United Kingdom did the same, ending the debate.

The American Cocker Spaniel breed still shares many traits with the English Cocker Spaniel. Although smaller than their English counterparts, American Cocker Spaniels are capable gun dogs. They have a natural desire to hunt, take to the water readily, and have the ability to sniff out and follow a scent trail. The American version of the Cocker Spaniel also makes a wonderful pet. These dogs know how to

Cocker Spaniel in 1878, and a breed club, the American Spaniel Club, was formed three years later.

However, over time American breeders focused on different qualities in their dogs than their English counterparts did. Some American owners began breeding more for size and appearance, and less for hunting ability. As a result, over time Cocker Spaniels in the United States became shorter, smaller, and had longer, silki-

have fun and will happily return any affection they receive.

BREED STANDARD FOR AMERICAN COCKER SPANIELS

The American Kennel Club, which is the breed standard authority for dogs in the United States, describes the American Cocker Spaniel as a "free and merry" dog with a "sturdy, compact body" and a "keen inclination to work." The ideal height of a mature male Cocker Spaniel is 15 inches (38 cm) tall at the withers (shoulders), while an adult female should be 14 inches (35.6 cm) tall.

A well-bred American Cocker Spaniel's head will be rounded, not flat, with clearly defined eyebrows, square jaws, and a broad muzzle. The eyeballs should be round, but the shape of the eye rims should be slightly almond-like in appearance. Eyes should look straight ahead; the iris of the eyes should be a dark brown. The expression on a Cocker

A purebred American Cocker Spaniel poses during a conformation show.

Spaniel's face should be intelligent, alert, soft, and appealing.

Cocker Spaniels should have a wide chest and a strong back that slopes slightly downward from the shoulders to the tail. The forelegs should be parallel, muscular, and set close to the body, while the hind legs should be strongly boned and powerful with clearly defined thighs. Feet should be compact, round, and turn neither in nor out. According to the breed standard, an American Cocker Spaniel's tail should be docked, or amputated.

A Cocker Spaniel's coat should be silky and flat. A wavy coat is acceptable in an American Cocker Spaniel, but a curly coat is undesirable and will be heavily penalized in the show ring. For purebred American Cocker Spaniels, four categories of coat color are permitted by the AKC breed standard:

FAST FACT

According to the AKC breed standard, a Cocker Spaniel that is well balanced in all areas is more desirable than a Cocker Spaniel with strongly contrasting good points and faults. The AKC's Web site lists the breed standards for both English and American Cocker Spaniels.

BLACK VARIETY: Black variety Cocker Spaniels can range from solid black to black-with-tan-points. Jet black is preferred. Brown or liver shades in a black coat are not desirable. A small amount of white on the chest and/or throat is permissible. However, white in any other location will disqualify an American Cocker Spaniel in the show ring.

ANY SOLID COLOR OTHER THAN BLACK (ASCOB): Cocker Spaniels that fall into the ASCOB category may have any solid color other than black, including (but not limited to) light cream, buff, brown, red, or brown with tan points. The color should be uniform, though lighter-colored feathering is allowed. A small amount of white on the chest and/or throat is permissible. However, white in any other location will disqualify a Cocker Spaniel in the show ring.

PARTI-COLOR VARIETY: Parti-color variety Cocker Spaniels may have two or more solid colors, one of which must be white. This may include black and white, red and white, and brown and white. Merle and roan Cocker Spaniels are also classified as parti-colors.

TAN POINTS: Cocker Spaniels may have tan points that range from the lightest cream to the darkest red. Tan points are restricted to 10 percent of the color or less and may be located in any of the following places a clear tan spot over each eye, on the sides of the muzzle and on the cheeks, on the underside of the ears, on all feet and/or legs, under the tail, and on the chest.

BREED STANDARD FOR ENGLISH COCKER SPANIELS

American and English Cocker Spaniels are not drastically different in appearance. Both breeds are sturdy and compact sporting dogs with similar coloring and markings. However, the AKC's breed standard for English Cocker Spaniels is slightly different

The English Cocker Spaniel is slightly larger than his American counterpart.

from the standard established for the American Cocker Spaniel.

One area of difference is size. The ideal height for a mature male English Cocker Spaniel is 16 to 17 inches (40.6 to 43.2 cm). Ideal height for an adult female is 15 to 16 inches (38 to 40.6 cm). The most desirable weight for English Cocker Spaniel males falls between 28 and 34 pounds (12.7 and 15.4 kg); females should weigh between 26 and 32 pounds (11.8 and 14.5 kg).

Another obvious difference is in the shape of the head. The English Cocker Spaniel's skull should be arched and slightly flattened when viewed from the side or front. These dogs also have a longer muzzle than their American counterparts. Their eyes are more oval-shaped than the eyes of the American Cocker Spaniel. The eyes are also set farther back in the English Cocker Spaniel's head.

The English Cocker Spaniel's coat is thick, but not as long and lustrous as the American Cocker Spaniel's coat. The hair on an English Cocker Spaniel's head should be short and fine, with medium-length hair on the body. An English Cocker Spaniel's hair should always be silky in texture and may be flat or slightly wavy. A roan coat is more common in the English Cocker Spaniel than in the American Cocker Spaniel.

CHAPTER THREE

Choosing the Right Cocker Spaniel

Once you've decided that the Cocker Spaniel is the right breed for you and your family, it will be time to find the perfect dog. As you begin this search, there are certain things that you should keep in mind. If you intend to show your Cocker Spaniel in conformation events, you will want to choose a dog that is as close to the standard for his breed as possible. A Cocker Spaniel that is too tall or short, has an unusual coat color or markings, or otherwise strays from the expected appearance is likely to be disqualified from competition.

Physical appearance should also be considered if you intend to breed your Cocker Spaniel. Choosing dogs that adhere closely to the standard of

A Cocker Spaniel will enjoy accompanying you practically anywhere.

perfection is the only way to preserve important characteristics of the breed, which is what responsible breeding is all about.

If you are looking for a family pet or a hunting companion, appearance is less important than your personal standards. A Cocker Spaniel's physical attributes have no effect on his temperament, intelligence, or ability to perform in the field.

Before you acquire any Cocker Spaniel, some factors that you should consider are the prospective dog's temperament, gender, age, and health:

TEMPERAMENT: Temperament is a major consideration. You want to choose a Cocker Spaniel that will be a good fit for your home, personality, and the role you have established for him. If you are looking for a family pet, you'll want a puppy or an adult dog that is good with children. If you are looking for a hunting dog or show dog, on the other hand, size, ability, and lineage are important.

When looking at a litter of puppies, the way they interact with each other will give you an idea of each dog's temperament. Put an open cardboard box into the puppies' play area and watch how they react. Brash puppies that lead the pack and step on the heads of their brothers and sisters to get to what is in their line of vision may turn into bold dogs that are difficult to control and train. Shy puppies that hang back and

Watching how a puppy interacts with his siblings can help you understand what he will be like as an adult dog.

avoid all of the action may eventually morph into distrustful dogs that bite or nip out of fear. For the beginning dog owner, the best choice is usually a puppy that falls somewhere in the middle. This type of dog is friendly and lively but not overly pushy. When interacting with littermates, he doesn't submit entirely. Yet he also doesn't seek to dominate everyone in his vicinity either. Cocker Spaniel puppies with this type of personality are usually the easiest to train.

Also, look for a puppy that is in good physical condition. His coat should be free from bald patches, and his skin should look pink and healthy. There should be no discharge from his eyes, ears, nose, or anus. His eyes should be bright and clear. The puppy should be able to walk and run with an even, balanced

Both male and female Cocker Spaniels can make great pets.

gait. If all these things check out, you may have found yourself the right Cocker Spaniel.

GENDER: When it comes to Cocker Spaniels, there is very little difference between males and females. Both are equally intelligent, affectionate, and trainable. A male Cocker Spaniel will have a natural instinct to mark his territory by urinating on objects. This behavior can be eliminated through training or by having the dog neutered. Female Cocker Spaniels do not mark their territory, but they may unintentionally soil their surroundings while in heat. A female Cocker Spaniel's bleeding is typically light, but could stain carpet or furniture. This problem can be eliminated if your female dog is spayed.

AGE: Deciding between a puppy and adult dog can be difficult. There are advantages and disadvantages to each. Puppies are cute and can be great fun to train, but they also require a lot of time and patience. If you do not properly socialize and train a puppy, he could grow into a huge problem. Adolescent or adult dogs, like those typically available for adoption at an animal shelter or breed rescue, may already be housebroken and trained to follow basic commands. You'll also have a better idea of the dog's temperament: with an adult dog, what you see is generally what you get. The drawback is that a fully grown Cocker Spaniel may be set in his ways. If the dog has never been around children, for example, he may not be comfortable around a young crowd. Adult dogs may also have bad habits that are hard to break.

HEALTH: Regardless of age and gender, it is important to find a healthy dog. If you choose a Cocker Spaniel that has a serious illness or a predisposition for certain health problems, you may be setting yourself up for heartbreak. A veterinary checkup is the best way to determine whether or not a dog is healthy. You can also look over the Cocker Spaniel yourself to get a feel for the dog's condition. Both the eyes and ears should be clear and free of discharge. The skin and coat should look clean and healthy; scabs, rashes, bald spots, and other issues could signal an infection or a serious skin condition. Finally, do not hesitate to ask the breeder if the dog's parents have been tested for hereditary problems that commonly affect Cocker Spaniels, such as progressive retinal atrophy, hip dysplasia, or hypothyroidism. Choosing a Cocker Spaniel

Cocker Spaniel puppies need time with their mother to grow properly. The breeder also needs time to start socializing the puppies and have them checked by a veterinarian. Most puppies will not be ready for a new home until they are at least eight to ten weeks old.

from parents who are certified as genetically problem-free does not guarantee that your puppy will be healthy, but it does make hereditary health issues much less likely.

ACQUIRING A COCKER SPANIEL

Finding a Cocker Spaniel should not be too difficult. They are among the most popular dog breeds in the United States, and can almost always be found wherever dogs are sold. Of course, that doesn't mean that you should not be selective when deciding where to purchase your Cocker Spaniel. Most pet stores are more concerned with making money than they are with selling the highest-

quality pets. If you want a purebred Cocker Spaniel, you are probably better off avoiding pet stores and looking for a responsible breeder who is dedicated to finding good homes for her puppies.

Responsible breeders understand the breed and choose their stock carefully. They do not breed dogs with hereditary conditions or inappropriate temperaments. A good breeder also spends money on visits to the veterinarian and vaccinations to keep the dogs they breed and their puppies healthy.

Older puppies and adult Cocker Spaniels can be found at animal shelters or breed rescues. It may be possible to adopt a Cocker Spaniel with AKC registration papers; surprisingly, almost one-third of all shelter dogs are purebred. Even without papers, many shelter dogs will make good pets. If you've decided that you'd rather have an older dog than a puppy, adoption can be very rewarding.

FINDING A RESPONSIBLE BREEDER

Many people breed Cocker Spaniels, but not every breeder is responsible. Those who do it for the money are less likely to take proper care of their animals. To avoid these sorts of unscrupulous breeders, look for breeders that are recommended by the American Kennel Club, the American Spaniel Club, or the English Cocker Spaniel Club of America. Breeders who are listed with these organizations are typically in good standing and follow a code of ethics.

Officers of local or regional breed clubs may be able to direct you to responsible breeders in your area who raise high-quality Cocker Spaniels as a hobby. Sometimes, such small breeding operations, even if not listed by AKC, will produce puppies that are just as good as those available from a larger breeder. The important things are that the breeder must be knowledgeable about the Cocker Spaniel breed standard, and must be willing to stand behind the health and temperament of the puppies they sell.

Of course, buying from a recommended breeder does not guarantee a good experience. Once you have identified a few prospective breeders, question each one about her methods and procedures until you find a breeder that you believe will be able to provide a puppy that meets your needs. You can ask to see a litter of her puppies, and, if possible, the dam and sire, prior to making a purchase. Most breeders will be willing to let you see puppies that are old enough for visitors. They'll also let you visit the place where the puppies are being raised.

QUESTIONS TO ASK A BREEDER

There are several questions that you can ask a prospective breeder to determine whether she is truly committed to breeding healthy Cocker Spaniel puppies. The following list is

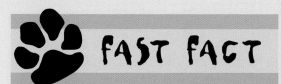

FAST FACT

There is usually very little difference between the price a novice breeder will charge for a Cocker Spaniel and the price an established breeder will charge.

a good starting point for anyone searching for a well-bred dog:

- Are you familiar with the Cocker Spaniel breed standard? *The answer should definitely be yes. Breeders who are not familiar with the standard cannot choose the best dams or sires and should not be running a breeding business.*
- How long have you been breeding Cocker Spaniels? *There is no wrong answer, but longer is almost always better.*
- Why did you decide to start breeding Cocker Spaniels? *The answer should not be "for the money." Almost any other answer is acceptable.*
- How many different breeds do you work with? *The best breeders usually concentrate on one or two breeds.*
- How often is the dam bred? *Anything more than once each year is irresponsible.*
- How old is the dam? *She should be at least two years old.*
- How did you choose the sire? *The sire should be chosen based on conformation to the breed standard and temperament.*
- Were genetic tests performed on the parents? *The answer should be*

Cocker Spaniel puppies are likely to grow up resembling their parents, like this American Cocker Spaniel father and son. If you like the way that a breeder's adult dogs look and act, chances are you'll be satisfied with one of their offspring.

Cocker Spaniel puppies are so cute that it's easy to fall in love with them, but not every pup will be right for you. Don't fall for the first pair of soft brown eyes that you see. Instead, handle and observe the pups for a while, then decide if one of them is the right animal companion. The puppy you choose should be clean, healthy, and confident.

yes. *Responsible breeders always have parents tested for hereditary problems that could be passed on to puppies.*

- How far back can you trace the parents' bloodlines? *There is no wrong answer, but the farther the better. Typically, a purebred dog will have at least a three-generation pedigree.*

- Will I be able to meet the par-ents? *You should be able to meet at least one of them, if not both.*

- Where do you raise your Cocker Spaniel puppies? *There is no wrong answer, but the best answer is "in my house."*

- Do you socialize the puppies? *The answer should be yes. Lack of early socialization can lead to serious behavioral problems later.*

- Are your puppies vaccinated? *Puppies should have their initial inoculations before being released to their new owners.*

- Have the puppies been checked for parasites? *All puppies should be checked and treated for worms and other parasites after they are weaned.*

- How much will a Cocker Spaniel puppy cost? *There is no wrong answer to this. However, you should expect to pay a significant sum if you are buying from a good breeder. The cost of a healthy purebred dog could range from $250 to several thousand dollars.*

- How long will I have to wait for a puppy? *Reputable breeders often have waiting lists. It is not unusual to have to wait several months for a purebred Cocker Spaniel pup.*

BUYING FROM A PET STORE

A pet store may not be the best place to purchase a Cocker Spaniel. Unlike responsible breeders, pet stores are in business for profit. Many of the dogs they sell come from puppy mills.

Puppy mills are kennels that breed large numbers of dogs under terrible conditions. In these settings, dogs are very rarely bred responsibly, and they are almost never given adequate love or medical attention. Females are usually bred every heat cycle until they can no longer carry puppies to term.

Very few of the puppies that come from these mills have been socialized properly. As a result, the puppies often have behavioral problems that make them difficult to train. Poor physical conditions are also common. Puppy mill Cocker Spaniels are likely to be underfed, riddled with parasites, and infected with kennel cough.

If you do decide to buy from a pet store, do your research first. There are some good pet stores, but they are relatively rare. Buying an unhealthy dog now can lead to heartbreak later. Furthermore, you wouldn't want to reward the inhumane treatment of animals.

Don't be surprised if the breeder has some questions for you as well. Some of the things they will want to know include why you want a dog, what you intend to do with the dog, and how you plan to care for the dog. It is important to answer these questions openly and honestly. Reputable breeders don't want to be intrusive or nosy. They just want to make sure their puppies are going to good homes.

ADOPTING A COCKER SPANIEL

The process of adopting a Cocker Spaniel from an animal shelter or rescue organization is similar to that of buying a puppy from a breeder. There are almost always fees to pay, but in most cases they don't exceed $100. This money typically goes toward the care and rescue of other dogs.

Shelters and rescue organizations also require an application from anyone who wants to adopt a pet. This application will ask questions about

FAST FACT

Some breed rescue groups will refund part of the adoption fee when you show proof that you've had your dog spayed or neutered.

your work schedule, living situation, and history with pets. Prospective Cocker Spaniel owners should be prepared to explain why they want a dog and what they plan to do once they take their new family member home.

Most animal shelters and rescue organizations reserve the right to reject applications at their discretion. However, rejections are very rare. The majority of adoption applications are approved without any problems. That said, adoption usually isn't a one-day process. Some shelters will take several days to review applications and prepare dogs for their new home.

CHAPTER FOUR

Responsible Cocker Spaniel Ownership

Owning a Cocker Spaniel comes with a great deal of responsibility. In addition to making sure that a pet is both healthy and happy, pet owners must meet basic requirements established by law. These include purchasing licensing and identification as well as complying with noise ordinances and littering laws. A responsible pet owner knows and obeys the local laws related to dog ownership.

Pet owners must also be considerate of neighbors and other members of the community. People will become annoyed if your Cocker Spaniel barks incessantly or leaves messes on someone's lawn. As a dog

Proper ID is essential in case your Cocker Spaniel wanders away from home.

owner, it is your responsibility to make sure your dog is under control and to clean up after your pet. Be respectful of the others who live in your community.

IDENTIFICATION

In most communities, dogs are required to wear collars and tags that identify their owners. Laws typically require that the tags include the owner's name, address, and zip code. Pet owners who live in these areas should follow the established rules to avoid citations and fines.

Even if you live in one of the few places where dogs don't need to wear tags, consider doing it anyway. According to the Humane Society,

Your Cocker Spaniel should wear a properly fitted collar that carries an ID tag.

one in three pets will become lost at some point during their lifetimes, and only 20 percent of lost pets without collar ID will be reunited with their owners. Making sure that your Cocker Spaniel has some form of identification greatly increases his chances of being returned.

In addition to collar tags, there are several other common identification methods: tattooing and microchip implantation. Both methods are considered permanent techniques. Tattooing is the older of the two techniques, but it is no more reliable than microchip identification.

Tattooed dogs are marked with a series of numbers. In most cases, these numbers are the same as the owner's telephone number or the dog's AKC registration number. Common locations for the tattoo include the belly and the inside of the thigh. However, the tattoo can be placed on other sections of the body as well.

Tattooing can be a very effective identification method, but there are drawbacks to the procedure. Over time, the tattoo can fade so much that it becomes unreadable. Registering the tattoo can also be confusing. Multiple registries need to be contacted and updated on a regular basis.

Pet owners who are uncomfortable with tattooing can opt for microchip implantation instead. This high-tech method is similar to tattooing in that it attaches dogs to their own unique number. The difference is that the identification is not topical. It exists within a computer chip that is implanted under the dog's skin. The chip is about the size of a grain of rice and is delivered via injection.

Lost dogs that have a microchip can be scanned with a special scanner and returned to their owners. The only drawback to this is that there are several different chips and scanners on the market. If a pet with

CHOOSING THE RIGHT COLLAR

When it comes time to buy a collar for your Cocker Spaniel, you will find that there are plenty of different styles to choose from. A traditional collar will work well for most dogs. However, there are occasions in which a special collar may work better.

Traditional Dog Collar: Traditional dog collars are usually made from leather, nylon, or woven cotton. This collar should fit snugly around your Cocker Spaniel's neck. If it is too loose, he could slip out of the collar. Don't make the collar too tight, however. You should be able to slip two fingers between your dog's neck and the collar without difficulty.

Harness: A harness is designed to fit around a dog's neck, over his shoulders, and behind his front legs. This type of collar works well for a Cocker Spaniel that pulls while on a leash, choking himself. A harness also gives the person walking the dog more control over the animal's movements.

Halter-style collar: A halter-style collar fits around the nose and over the back of a dog's head. It resembles a horse halter and offers superior control over your dog's movements. Halter-style collars work especially well for Cocker Spaniels that try to pull ahead or wander away while walking on a leash.

Chain-slip Collars: Also known as choke chains, chain-slip collars are intended for strong-willed dogs that cannot be trained with a traditional dog collar. These collars are not typically recommended, or needed, for Cocker Spaniels. In most cases, patience and a halter-style collar are all that is needed to train a Cocker to walk correctly.

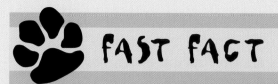

FAST FACT

Including the phrase "needs medication" on a dog's identification tag can encourage the prompt return of a lost pet.

a microchip ends up at a shelter with an incompatible scanner, there is a chance the chip will not be discovered. There have also been cases in which the chip has moved inside a dog's body, making it unreadable.

LICENSING REQUIREMENTS

Many countries require pet owners to purchase licenses for canines, and the United States is no exception. Every municipality within the United States requires pet owners to register and license their dogs. In most cases, this license must be renewed each year.

The cost of a license varies by location and by place of purchase. Licenses can usually be purchased from the local courthouse. They may also be available from local veterinarians.

In many places, you can get a discount by purchasing a license early in the year. Some cities also have reduced fees for dogs that have been spayed or neutered. Discounts may also apply if your dog has permanent

identification, such as a tattoo or microchip.

Failure to get a license is considered a misdemeanor offense in many places and typically results in a fine. To ensure compliance, many local governments send officials door-to-door to look for unlicensed animals. Pet owners who want to avoid legal hassles should carefully follow the licensing requirements established in their area.

COMMON LEGAL ISSUES

Failure to properly license a dog isn't the only thing that can get a Cocker Spaniel owner into trouble. Barking, trespassing, littering, and biting can also create legal problems.

It is up to Cocker Spaniel owners to keep the barking of their canine companions under control. Many towns and cities have ordinances

FAST FACT

Many breed registries and clubs, including the American Kennel Club, encourage pet owners to get a registered tattoo or microchip implant so that dogs can be identified. The owners of some high-quality show dogs have DNA profiles of their dogs created, but this practice remains rare for pets.

regulating noise. These laws typically take effect at night, when most people want to sleep. These regulations limit the loudness and the duration of sounds coming from residences and businesses. A dog that barks for an extended period at night may well be in violation of noise ordinances. If neighbors complain to the police, that dog's owner may be slapped with a citation or fine. Repeat offenders may even have their dogs taken away.

Allowing a Cocker Spaniel to trespass on someone else's property is another recipe for trouble. If the dog destroys anything or makes a mess, the owner can be held financially responsible for the damage. To avoid trouble, owners should be vigilant about keeping their dogs in their own yards. Cleaning up after any messes that a Cocker Spaniel leaves behind is also important. The fines for not picking up a dog's waste can be considerable.

Barking dogs don't belong in residential neighborhoods. Your Cocker Spaniel will have to be properly trained and socialized so that he does not bark excessively. Otherwise, you may be fined for violating local noise ordinances.

The most common legal problem pet owners face involves biting. According to the Centers for Disease Control and Prevention, dogs bite about 4.7 million people in the United States every year. Medical treatment is required in more than 15 percent of these cases. Half of the people treated are children.

Like everyone who owns a dog, Cocker Spaniel owners have a responsibility to minimize the chance that their pet will bite someone. The consequences of dog biting can be severe. Dogs that cause serious injury may be put to death, and owners may face significant legal and financial penalties.

The majority of dog bites happen on the owner's property, so posting a warning sign there is a good idea. Owners should also use a leash when walking their dogs. Extra precautions should be taken when a dog has displayed aggressive tendencies. In that case a responsible owner will find a way to control and correct the dog's behavior. This may require obedience training or the help of a behavioral specialist.

SPAYING OR NEUTERING

Spaying or neutering is another responsibility that should not be overlooked. These surgeries prevent unwanted pregnancies and help pets live longer, healthier lives. Spaying a young female can prevent uterine, ovarian, and breast cancer. Neutering a young male can reduce, and practically eliminate, the risk of testicular cancer and prostate disease. Spaying or neutering also reduces the incidence of certain problem behaviors, such as roaming or territorial marking by males or hormone-induced mood swings in females.

Cocker Spaniels can be spayed or neutered at six months of age. Both surgeries are relatively inexpensive and can be performed by any licensed veterinarian. Whenever possible, females should be spayed before their first heat cycle.

When spaying or neutering a dog, most vets now use laser surgery, although some continue to practice the more traditional scalpel-and-suture method. Laser surgery is preferable because recovery time is

FAST FACT

Some homeowner's insurance policies provide coverage for dog bites that occur on the property; others do not. Check with your insurance provider to find out whether dog-bite coverage is available as part of your policy.

FAST FACT

Spaying is a term used for the surgical removal of a female dog's ovaries, fallopian tubes, and uterus. *Neutering* is the term used for the surgical removal of a male dog's testicles.

faster. Regardless of method, a pet's pain can be controlled through anesthesia and medication.

As with any medical procedure, spaying or neutering carries some risks. Complications may arise from the use of anesthesia. Internal bleeding or infection is also a concern.

Despite the risks, there are only two good reasons to refrain from spaying or neutering: breeding or showing. In the case of breeding, the explanation is obvious. In the case of showing, the explanation involves American Kennel Club rules. Conformation shows were originally developed to showcase breeding stock, so the AKC does not allow dogs that have been sterilized to participate in AKC-sanctioned conformation shows.

PET INSURANCE

Typically, pet insurance—which reimburses policyholders for veterinary expenses—covers the costs of spaying or neutering a dog. Most pet insurance policies also provide coverage for other surgeries, as well as hospitalization, illnesses, accidents, and prescriptions. Some policies cover preventive care, such as annual checkups, teeth cleaning, parasite control, and health screenings.

Pet insurance policies can be purchased from various sources. Veterinarians don't normally sell policies, but they may be able to recommend a carrier. An Internet search can also turn up hundreds of companies and organizations that provide health and life insurance plans for pets. Two of the best-known organizations are the American Society for the Prevention of Cruelty to Animals (ASPCA) and the American Kennel Club. Each offers nationally recognized insurance plans with varying levels of coverage.

The plans offered by the ASPCA, the AKC, and other pet insurance carriers are similar to health insurance plans for people. The pet owner pays an annual premium, the size of which depends on the insurance carrier, the level of coverage, the age of the pet, the geographic location, and other factors. Typically, pet insurance policies have a deductible, which means that the insurance carrier begins paying out claims only after the pet owner has spent a certain

Pet insurance first became available more than 30 years ago. Hundreds of companies now provide insurance coverage for dogs, cats, and other pets. But before you sign up for a plan, make sure you know what procedures and conditions are covered and what are not.

amount of money toward the dog's care. Most plans also include co-pays for each visit to the veterinarian.

To make sure that they are getting the best deal, Cocker Spaniel owners should comparison-shop before buying an insurance policy. In addition to considering premiums, deductibles, and co-pays, pet owners are well advised to find out about exclusions and gaps in coverage. Every policy has some sort of exclusion. Most involve preexisting conditions. However, some policies won't pay for preventive care or elective procedures, such as teeth cleaning or genetic testing.

Another factor worth investigating is the method by which the insurance carrier pays out claims. Some pay veterinarians directly, but most require the owner to pay up front and wait for reimbursement. Knowing which method is used before signing up for a policy is always a good idea.

A final consideration for Cocker Spaniel owners is cost. Although a pet insurance plan can be a smart financial investment for some people, these policies do not pay off for everyone. In fact, it may cost more to pay the premiums, deductibles, and co-pays than it does to pay for veterinary care out of pocket.

CHAPTER FIVE

The Best Possible Beginning

Before bringing a Cocker Spaniel home, the house and family must be prepared to receive the new addition. The first thing a Cocker Spaniel will want to do is explore his new space and meet everyone in it. Creating a safe environment that is full of love will ensure the best possible beginning.

PUPPY-PROOFING YOUR HOME

Cocker Spaniels are curious, playful dogs. They will chew on or play with just about anything they can reach. Unfortunately, some of these things can be very dangerous to your new pet, especially if they can be broken or swallowed. Every room in the house may contain something

Take time to make your house safe for a dog before you bring your Cocker Spaniel home.

hazardous for a dog. Cocker Spaniels are small enough to get into relatively confined spaces, and curious enough to get into trouble. For this reason, you should puppy-proof your home before bringing your Cocker Spaniel home.

The best approach is to get down on the floor and view each space as your Cocker Spaniel would. Are there small items within reach? Is there enough room for him to squeeze behind furniture and chew on electrical cords? Are there poisonous houseplants on low tables or windowsills? Are there window screens that might tear or fall out under the pressure of his paws? All of these things must be considered and addressed.

Here are some specific areas that must be cleared of potential hazards before you allow your Cocker Spaniel to explore them:

KITCHEN: The tasty smells that waft from kitchens, and the fact that your dog probably will be eating there, make this room a favorite for most Cocker Spaniels. Putting child locks on cabinets that contain food, trash, and cleaning supplies may be the only way to keep him from eating things he shouldn't. If your kitchen trashcan is not located inside a cabinet, make sure it's sturdy enough

that your Cocker Spaniel can't easily knock it over.

LIVING ROOM AND FAMILY ROOM: Your home's living spaces will generally contain a wide range of things that will fit inside a Cocker Spaniel's mouth. Remote controls, knickknacks, beverage coasters, magazines, and other items will almost certainly catch the attention of a bored puppy. Make sure they're put out of reach. Electrical cords should be hidden, taped down, or covered with a material made specifically for this purpose.

Your Cocker Spaniel will try to chew electrical cords if he can reach them. Raise cords out of reach or block them from your dog.

BEDROOMS: The typical bedroom contains a variety of potential hazards for a Cocker Spaniel. Some, like electrical cords, are obvious. Others, however, are not. These include jewelry and laundry. Cocker Spaniels can be clever enough to get things left on top of low dressers and night tables. Keep earrings, necklaces, and other jewelry in a box that's out of reach. Cocker Spaniels have also been known to ingest socks and other small items of clothing, which can create an obstruction that requires emergency surgery. All clothing—clean and otherwise—should be kept in drawers or behind closed doors where a dog can't get to it.

If your Cocker Spaniel shares the house with a cat, make sure that he cannot get to the cat's litter. If he swallows the litter, he could choke or suffer from impacted intestines.

BATHROOMS: The most obvious hazard in a bathroom is the toilet, which your Cocker Spaniel may see as a water source. However, water in a toilet bowl may contain harmful bacteria like E. coli or salmonella, or the water may contain harmful chemicals from toilet bowel cleaners or refreshers. Teach family members to keep toilet lids down; if necessary, toilet lid locks can keep persistent dogs out of the bowl.

As in the kitchen, child locks should be placed on bathroom cabinets to keep curious puppies away from cleaning supplies, medications, and other potential hazards. Countertops should also be kept free of makeup, curling irons, hair driers, and other beauty products. If a puppy pulls these things off a counter, he could be hit on the head. There is also a chance of electrocu-

Make sure that your backyard is safely fenced, and that it does not contain plants that could make your dog sick if he ingests them.

tion if he chews on something that is plugged into a wall outlet.

GARAGE: This area of the house often contains antifreeze, cleaning supplies, pesticides, and other substances that are very toxic for Cocker Spaniels. These products should be locked up or kept well out of reach. The same is true of sharp tools and items that are small enough to swallow.

YARD: Potential backyard hazards include garden tools and children's toys. These items should be picked up before a Cocker Spaniel is allowed to roam freely. Plants are equally dangerous because many are toxic to Cocker Spaniels. Azaleas, daffodils, holly, nightshade, ivy, and baby's breath are just a few of the common backyard plants that can poison a puppy. (The American Society for the Prevention of Cruelty to Animals provides a comprehensive listing of toxic plants online at www.aspca.org/pet-care/poison-control/plants.)

Pools, fences, kennels, and similar structures should also be made secure. An unsupervised puppy could fall into a pool or become entangled within a pool cover. Fences and kennels pose entirely different problems. If the fence or gate isn't sturdy or flush with the ground, your Cocker Spaniel may try to wriggle his way out of an enclosure. As he does, he could get hurt on a jagged piece of fence. If he manages to escape, your pet could wander off into the street, get hit by a car, and end up with far worse than a cut or minor injury.

CREATING A SECURE SPACE FOR YOUR COCKER SPANIEL

Before bringing a puppy home, it is a good idea to decide where the puppy may and may not go within the house. A Cocker Spaniel will want to investigate every inch of his new world as soon as he arrives. If certain rooms are off limits to him, he should know that immediately. You can create solid boundaries by keeping doors closed or blocking entryways with a baby gate or other obstruction.

Even if you want to give your Cocker Spaniel the run of the house, it's important to create a small and secure space to help him settle into his new home. This space could be a laundry room, mudroom, or another area with puppy-friendly floors. If your house doesn't have such a

room, you can use an exercise pen. These pens are small enough to be placed in any room, but large enough for a puppy to have space to move around and play.

Whenever a puppy is left alone for an extended period, he should be kept in his safe place. This not only provides a sense of security for the puppy, it also prevents him from getting into trouble when nobody is around to watch. To make being left alone easier, include his water dish, a blanket, and some fun chew toys in his safe place.

Most Cocker Spaniels enjoy having a plastic or wire crate that can serve as a sort of bedroom. Like other den animals, Cocker Spaniels like having a small, comfy space that is all their own. The crate should be big enough for a puppy to grow into, but not too big. A medium-sized crate of 30 inches (76 cm) is ideal for most Cocker Spaniels. At minimum, the crate should be large enough to permit your dog to stand up and turn around.

PREPARING YOUR FAMILY

Preparing your family for the new arrival is just as important as preparing your home. You must establish ground rules so that everyone is on the same page when it comes to how the puppy will be treated.

Consistency is the key to raising a happy, healthy Cocker Spaniel.

Everyone in the household should sit down together to discuss how common situations should be handled. Specific subjects to talk about include what the puppy will eat, when the puppy will eat, and what steps will be taken to train and socialize the puppy. Responsibilities should also be doled out at this time. Establish who will feed the puppy, who will walk the puppy, and who will take time to train the puppy each day.

If there are children in the house, there should also be a brief education session. Overly enthusiastic roughhousing can easily injure puppies. It is essential that everyone in the house understand how a puppy should be handled.

BRINGING YOUR COCKER SPANIEL HOME

Before the big day, assemble everything your puppy will need when he arrives. Make sure that you have food, dog dishes, a small collar, a leash, toys for the puppy to play with, and a crate in which to train and transport the puppy. Having carpet cleaner, stain remover, and other cleaning supplies on hand is also a good idea. Puppies always have accidents in the first few weeks.

A properly sized plastic or wire crate can help you house-train your Cocker Spaniel. Puppies do not like to urinate where they sleep. If the crate is too large, the puppy will be able to make a mess in one corner and comfortably sleep in another.

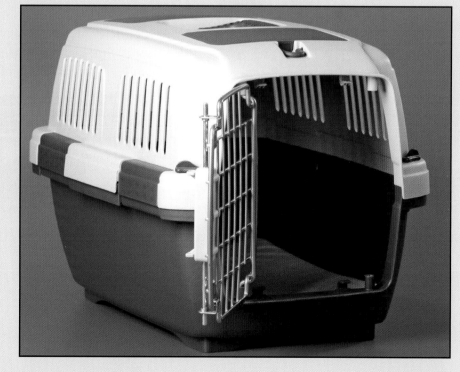

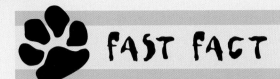

FAST FACT

Always be kind, gentle, and affectionate with your puppy. If you are not, he may be come frightened of you or grow into an aggressive dog.

If not cleaned up properly, the smell will encourage even more accidents.

The final item you will need is a list of last-minute questions to ask the breeder or shelter employees. Make sure you find out the puppy's vaccination schedule, diet, and feeding times. If you are picking up an older dog, you will want to get this information as well as find out about the dog's favorite toys and his ability to follow commands.

THE FIRST NIGHT

It will be exciting for everyone when your new Cocker Spaniel arrives at your home for the first time. It will require some effort on your part, but take things slowly so that he is not overwhelmed. This is especially important if you're bringing home a puppy. This will all be new to him, and he may be nervous about being in a strange place without his litter-mates.

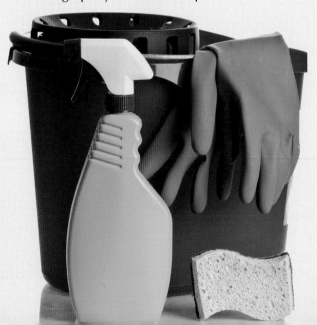

Have cleaning supplies on hand before your puppy comes home. When accidents aren't cleaned up quickly and thoroughly, dogs tend to return and go potty in the same spot.

Before doing anything else, give your Cocker Spaniel a few minutes to explore his new surroundings. Encourage him with gentle touches and light praise. After he's had a chance to check things out, he'll be ready to meet the rest of the family. Introductions should be made slowly and kindly. The puppy will feel much less overwhelmed if he gets to meet everyone in turn instead of all at once.

Your Cocker Spaniel puppy will need many bathroom breaks during the day. Try to take him out every hour, so that he can get used to going in the area of the yard that you designate as his "potty place." Don't be surprised if he has an accident or two in the house. It will take time for your Cocker Spaniel to understand where he should and shouldn't do his business. Each time you are able to get him to go to the bathroom outside, give him lots of praise and attention so that he knows you are pleased with this behavior.

Your puppy will enjoy playing with family members and exploring the home, but at some point he'll probably succumb to exhaustion. This is completely normal. Puppies play hard, but they also spend a lot of time sleeping. If your new friend wants to take a nap, let him. He might not get very much sleep when night finally rolls around.

A puppy's first night in a new place is often rough, particularly if the puppy is used to sleeping with his littermates. The experience of being alone at night can be very traumatic. To let everyone know how much he's suffering, the puppy may cry and whine for hours. His goal is to attract someone who is willing to comfort and play with him. Whatever you do, don't fall for it. It's okay to get up several times to let your puppy outside the first night, but you shouldn't get up just to comfort him. If you do, he'll learn that crying and whining are the best ways to get attention throughout the night.

THE FIRST FEW MONTHS

The first few months of Cocker Spaniel ownership will be both exciting and frustrating. There will be plenty of fun as you watch your new pet grow and discover his surroundings. But there may also be times when your puppy tests your patience and makes you wonder why you ever wanted a Cocker Spaniel. When you feel this way, remember that you made the commitment to owning a pet, and that your puppy will need lots of love, patience, affection, and understanding during this period to grow into a happy and healthy dog.

Make things easier on both you and your puppy by establishing regular feeding schedules, exercise times, and bathroom breaks. You should also work on basic obedience training every day. If you are patient and consistent, your wild puppy will eventually become a well-trained, well-behaved adult.

As your Cocker Spaniel grows, you will notice changes in his behav-ior. One week he may seem to have grasped your rules; the next week could be full of daily battles. This erratic behavior is completely nor-mal. All dogs go through different stages in their cognitive development during their first year of life. The rate at which a Cocker Spaniel devel-ops will vary from dog to dog, and is

You'll find that a Cocker Spaniel puppy has bountiful energy. Your task will be to make sure he expends that energy in useful ways. A bored Cocker Spaniel is more likely to make mischief or destroy household items by chewing them apart.

often dependent on environment, genetics, and testing. The following growth and cognitive development schedule offers an indication of what you can expect during your Cocker Spaniel's first year:

EIGHT TO TWELVE WEEKS: A reputable breeder will not allow you to take one of her purebred puppies until he's eight to ten weeks old. By eight weeks of age, a Cocker Spaniel puppy's brain is fully developed. The puppy should be socializing more with humans than with members of his canine pack. He should also be weaned and fully aware of where his food and water dishes are.

THIRTEEN TO SIXTEEN WEEKS: Cocker Spaniels between thirteen and sixteen weeks are considered adolescents. They are more likely than younger puppies to follow basic commands, but they also like to test boundaries. At this age, Cocker Spaniel puppies begin to associate praise and punishment with certain behaviors.

SEVENTEEN WEEKS TO SIX MONTHS: Dominant traits are fully established during this period. At six months of age, Cocker Spaniels reach sexual maturity. At this point, your Cocker Spaniel should be housebroken and able to understand basic commands ("sit," "stay," "down," and "come").

SIX MONTHS TO ONE YEAR: This is the final growing stage for most Cocker Spaniels. By the time these dogs are a year old, they will nearly have reached their full height. Your dog should be well trained and fully assimilated into the household at this point.

Spending time and using consistent training methods during your Cocker Spaniel's first year of life will help him become a well-behaved adult dog.

SOCIALIZATION

The average Cocker Spaniel is friend-ly and fun-loving. Dogs of this breed usually get along well with both people and other animals. To make sure that your dog develops a good temperament, you need to introduce him to unfamiliar people, animals, surroundings, and situations.

Your puppy's socialization should have started before you picked him up from the breeder. The most criti-cal period for socialization is during the first twelve weeks of a dog's life. This is when puppies form their impression of the world. If socialized properly, puppies will grow into happy, healthy dogs that love people and other animals. If not socialized properly, puppies may grow into shy, distrustful dogs that bite out of fear. Dogs that are improperly socialized can also be difficult to train.

Breeders usually begin the socialization process by getting the puppies used to being handled and introducing them to other people and animals. After you bring home your Cocker Spaniel, you'll need to continue this process. Try to introduce your puppy to many differ-ent people every week. The more human contact a puppy has, the more likely he is to be comfortable around people later in life. The same is true of other animals. Similarly,

(Left) It's important for your dog to learn how to interact peacefully with other friendly animals, just as this English Cocker Spaniel and Miniature Pinscher are doing. (Opposite) Regular walks through the neighborhood provide a great opportunity to safely expose your young Cocker Spaniel to new people and situations.

puppies should periodically be introduced to new experiences. Doing this will make situations such as trips to the vet, obedience classes, and rides in the car less scary.

The following tips will help you socialize your Cocker Spaniel properly during his first year of life:

- Introduce your puppy to new experiences gradually, so that he is not overwhelmed.
- Do not force your Cocker Spaniel to approach something that frightens him. Encourage him slowly and kindly.
- Introduce your Cocker Spaniel to loud sounds from a distance, so that he is not alarmed or over-whelmed.
- Take short rides in the car and make them pleasant. This will make trips to the groomer or vet less scary later on.
- Make sure that everyone treats your Cocker Spaniel with respect.

One bad experience with a stranger or houseguest could make your dog distrust people.

- Consider enrolling in a socialization class so that your puppy can play with other dogs in a safe environment.
- Feed your Cocker Spaniel a treat, pet him, and talk to him in a soothing voice when he is near a household appliance that frightens him, such as a vacuum cleaner or hair dryer. This will help him feel more at ease.
- Reward your puppy with praise and affection when he reacts appropriately to a new experience.

Make every effort to keep introductions fun for the puppy and make sure that he always feels safe. Positive experiences will help your Cocker Spaniel turn into a well-adjusted dog. Negative experiences will have the opposite effect.

CHAPTER SIX

Nutrition, Exercise, Grooming, and Training

It can be great fun to watch a Cocker Spaniel puppy grow to maturity. The period between six months and two years of age is especially enjoyable. Each day will bring new experiences for both you and your dog. However, this period can also be challenging, as your growing Cocker Spaniel will constantly test his boundaries. Proper training, combined with good nutrition, plentiful exercise, and regular grooming will help turn your Cocker Spaniel puppy into a healthy, well-behaved adult dog.

PUPPY NUTRITION

During their first few weeks of life, Cocker Spaniel puppies receive all of the nutrition they need from their

American Cocker Spaniels need regular grooming in order to look their best.

mother's milk. When the puppies are three to four weeks old, the breeder will begin feeding them solid food. By the time you pick up a puppy from the breeder, he should be fully weaned.

To develop properly, Cocker Spaniel puppies should be fed a diet that is high in protein, fat, calcium, and phosphorus. This combination supports the development of bones, teeth, muscles, and tissues. It also gives puppies the energy they need to keep going throughout the day. To make sure your puppy is eating the right amount and type of food for his size and age, maintain the diet and feeding schedule recommended by the breeder.

If you do decide to change the brand or type of food that your puppy is eating, do so gradually. Changing your puppy's diet suddenly could upset his digestive system. Instead, begin by replacing two tablespoons of the old food with two tablespoons of the new food at each feeding. Slowly increase the amount of new food versus old food each day until the meal consists of only the new food.

For puppies that eat store-bought food, there are three basic feeding options: dried kibble, canned food, and semi-moist food. Dried kibble is usually recommended over canned food or semi-moist food. Canned food often contains a lot of fat and water. Some canned food is more than 70 percent water. Semi-moist food, though palatable, is usually high in sugar. Dried kibble, on the other hand, has less fat, less sugar, and in many cases more nutrients. Other benefits of dried kibble include its lower cost and its ability to help reduce tartar buildup on a puppy's teeth.

Some Cocker Spaniel owners prefer to make their pet's food themselves, rather than purchasing dog food in the store. Homemade

When you purchase a dog from a breeder, ask her for food recommendations. Your veterinarian may also have suggestions about commercial food brands that would be good for your Cocker Spaniel.

Feeding Schedules

Cocker Spaniels have a healthy appetite, and it's a good idea to develop a regular feeding schedule for your pet. Free feeding, or leaving food out 24 hours per day for your dog to nibble at whenever he wants, is not a good idea, as it can to lead to obesity and other health problems. Scheduled feeding, on the other hand, allows you to control when and how much your Cocker Spaniel eats.

Feeding Schedule for Puppies: Young Cocker Spaniel puppies should eat at least four small meals throughout the day—one in the morning, two in the afternoon, and one at night. Each meal should be given at approximately the same time each day. At six months of age, Cocker Spaniels only need to be fed three times each day: in the morning, at noon, and at night.

Feeding Schedule for Adult Dogs: Adult dogs do not need to eat as frequently as puppies. At about 10 months your Cocker Spaniel's feedings can be reduced to once or twice per day. Feedings can occur in the morning or at night. If your pet is fed twice per day, he should eat the first meal in the morning and the second at night.

Feeding Schedule for Senior Dogs: A senior Cocker Spaniel's dietary needs may change, but in most cases there is no need to deviate from the schedule he's followed as an adult dog. As your senior Cocker Spaniel slows down, he'll need fewer calories, so you may want to cut back on the amount he eats so that he maintains a healthy weight. If you have difficulty getting an older pet to eat, try offering several smaller meals each day.

food diets can be great if the food is prepared properly. The problem is that it can be difficult to create meals with the proper proportions of nutrients. It can also be time-consuming to cook for your Cocker Spaniel every day. There are many good books and Web sites dedicated to home-cooked or raw food pet diets. Before you decide to try this option, consult with your veterinarian to make sure your Cocker Spaniel puppy gets the right nutrients for his size and age.

Whatever food you choose for your Cocker Spaniel, meat should be the first ingredient listed. Ideally, two of the first three ingredients should be meats. Don't be fooled by the term "meat by-products." That refers to parts of slaughtered animals that would not be considered good enough for human consumption. By-products include such things as feathers, feet, intestines, hair, beaks, and ground-up bones. They can also include sawdust or wood shavings, meat from animals killed on a highway ("roadkill"), and the rendered carcasses of dogs that have died from disease or been euthanized. Meat by-products have little nutritional value, and should not be among the first three ingredients.

ADULT COCKER SPANIEL NUTRITION

Small breed dogs, such as Cocker Spaniels, often reach their adult weight faster than larger breeds. To prevent overgrowth, which can result in health complications like hip dysplasia and arthritis, many veterinarians recommend switching Cocker Spaniels from puppy food to adult food when they are between six and twelve months old. Your veterinarian will tell you when it is time to make this change; it will depend on your dog's size and overall proportion.

Nutrition for an adult Cocker Spaniel is just as important as nutrition for a puppy. To maintain their energy levels and build healthy bones and muscles, adult Cocker Spaniels need a diet that is high in protein

READING DOG FOOD LABELS

The law requires pet food manufacturers to provide a clear label and ingredient list on each container of dog food. Learning how to read these labels and lists will help you choose the right food for your Cocker Spaniel.

To start, the label should contain a stamp of approval from the Association of American Feed Control Officials (AAFCO). Food that does not have the AAFCO stamp of approval is probably lacking in proper vitamins and minerals.

The ingredient list should also be clearly displayed. Ingredient lists include every ingredient that was used to make the food. Animal proteins should always be the number-one ingredient. Whole meats are preferable. Proteins derived from animal by-products such as lips, tendons, and feet do not provide the right nutrition for any dog.

Foods that use a grain or corn base are also unsuitable. Although it is okay for these ingredients to be included in the food, they should never be the number-one ingredient. Such foods do not contain the proper amount of protein or fatty acids.

from meats. Fats are also important for the same reason. Animal fats, such as chicken fat, tallow, and lard, provide energy. Fats from plant sources, such as safflower oil, soybean oil, and sunflower oil, keep the skin and coat healthy. Adult Cocker Spaniels also need some carbohydrates in their diet. Carbs can come from cooked corn, wheat, oats, barley, potatoes, and rice.

The final part of complete diet is fiber. Fermentable fiber, such as beet pulp, can promote a healthy

intestinal tract and reduce the risk of diarrhea.

As adult Cocker Spaniels grow and settle into their roles, their dietary needs change. Young adults, sporting dogs, and hunting dogs need more food and different types of food than older dogs that spend the bulk of their time on the couch. You can address your dog's dietary needs with your veterinarian.

EXERCISE

Cocker Spaniels are sporting dogs, and need a certain amount of exercise to maintain health and happiness. One of the best ways to make sure your Cocker Spaniel gets the exercise he needs is by taking him for regular walks. Dogs should be walked at least once each day, and preferably twice. Ten to 15 minutes is usually sufficient, though most Cocker Spaniels will be happy to walk longer. They love to sniff out new trails and take in the sights and sounds.

Other physical activities that Cocker Spaniels enjoy include running, jumping, hunting, and retrieving. You can jog with your Cocker Spaniel or, if you have a fenced-in backyard, set aside some time each day for him to play "fetch" with a tennis ball. This will give your dog a chance to stretch his legs and enjoy another favorite activity: retrieving. You can also enter your Cocker Spaniel in agility competitions, or train him to hunt and retrieve. Regular activity will prevent him from becoming obese, and enable your pet to avoid the health problems associated with that condition.

No matter what exercise you choose, it is important to keep an eye on your pet the entire time. Cocker Spaniels can overdo it when they are having fun. If your dog

looks tired or hurt, stop the exercise immediately. You should also make sure your dog stays hydrated with plenty of fresh water.

GROOMING

For a Cocker Spaniel, regular grooming is almost as important as good nutrition and daily exercise. Cocker Spaniels have long, luxurious coats that need frequent maintenance to remain clean and free of tangles. From the time he is a puppy, your pet should be brushed at least every two to three days, and preferably every day. He will also need to be bathed every three to six weeks depending on the length of his coat and tendency to get dirty. Nail, ear, and dental care are also important aspects of grooming. You can perform these tasks at home or enlist the help of a groomer or veterinarian.

At first your Cocker Spaniel will probably not be thrilled with grooming, but he will eventually get used to the process. If you are kind and gentle, he may even grow to enjoy the time you spend together. Regular brushing will help make the process more pleasant. If his coat has been

Your Cocker Spaniel will look forward to taking regular walks with you.

neglected, your Cocker Spaniel will not appreciate being forced to sit still while you painfully tear knots, tangles, and mats. The important thing is that you attend to your pet regularly to keep him clean and healthy.

BRUSHING: You can buy several different types of brushes and combs to groom your Cocker Spaniel. A soft bristle brush works well on the short coat and delicate skin of a puppy.

Slicker brushes with wire bristles or pin brushes with plastic-tipped bristles are ideal for adult Cocker Spaniels. A double-sided comb, which has wide teeth on one end and fine teeth on the other, makes a good finishing tool for dogs of any age. Such a comb works especially well on the thicker parts of a Cocker Spaniel's coat.

The best place to begin brushing is the head and ears. The back, legs,

A grooming table can be very helpful when it comes to properly brushing and clipping your Cocker Spaniel's coat.

chest, and belly can be done next. First, brush against the direction of hair growth, as this will loosen dead hairs. Then brush in the opposite direction to remove as much of the loose hair as possible. Try to get down to your pet's skin without scratching him.

If you encounter a stubborn knot or mat in the coat, do not tear or tug at it with the brush. You are much better off trying to break it apart with your fingers, using a detangling solution. You can also use a special dematting tool, which is available in pet stores. If all else fails, remove the mat by placing a comb between the mat and the dog's skin and using scissors to cut off the matted hair just above the comb.

BATHING: When it is time for your Cocker Spaniel to have a bath, make sure to first brush his coat carefully. Water makes matted hair very hard, so any mats or tangles in your pet's fur will be almost impossible to comb through or remove after he's been bathed. Knots and tangles also have a tendency to retain dirt and shampoo. They can defeat the purpose of the bath by making your pet smell bad or feel itchy if they are not removed before bathing.

After your pet has been thoroughly brushed, he is ready to be bathed. You may be able to bathe a puppy or small Cocker Spaniel in a sink or laundry tub. For an adult dog, the bathtub is probably the most practical option. You do not need any fancy equipment. A source of lukewarm water, a dog shampoo and conditioner, a hose with a spray attachment, a towel, and a hair dryer will get the job done.

Start by wetting your Cocker Spaniel's hair thoroughly from his neck to his tail. Be careful not to splash water in his face and try not to get his head wet until last. Dog's don't like to get their head wet, and

Gather all of your bathing supplies before you start. You don't want to leave your Cocker Spaniel in the tub while you're searching for something you forgot.

A hose with a spray attachment makes rinsing the lather out of your Cocker Spaniel's coat much easier.

will try to shake off the water when they do. When his coat is wet, begin working in the shampoo, moving down his torso and legs to the tail.

When your Cocker Spaniel is thoroughly lathered in shampoo, begin rinsing the soap out with luke-warm water. Rinse well, because any shampoo that is left behind will irritate his skin. After he's been rinsed, apply conditioner to detangle the coat and soothe his skin before rinsing once more.

After this, you can wet his head and face. Cotton balls can be placed in his ears to keep water out of his ear canals. Work shampoo carefully on his head, taking care not to get any soap in his eyes or mouth, then rinse it out thoroughly. When you've finished, quickly throw a towel over him to stop him from shaking the water off his coat. Dry his head and ears first, then gently towel off his body. Don't rub too hard, or you may create mats in his coat.

FAST FACT

When bathing your Cocker Spaniel, it's a good idea to dilute the pet shampoo with water before using it on his coat. Diluted shampoo will lather up more quickly, and will be easier to rinse out of his coat. Use an empty bottle to mix; aim for approximately 10 percent shampoo and 90 percent water.

You can let your Cocker Spaniel air dry after his bath, but it is much more beneficial to use a blow dryer. This will allow you to brush out any tangles or waves that appear as your pet dries. Keep your blow dryer on the lowest setting to avoid scorching your Cocker Spaniel's sensitive skin. It is also a good idea to blow the air in the direction of hair growth to get rid of any hair loosened by the bath. If you do let him air dry, don't let him out of the house until he's completely dry. A damp coat is more likely to pick up dirt and grime.

COAT TRIMMING: Maintaining a Cocker Spaniel's beautiful flowing coat requires regular trimming. You may want to enlist the services of a professional groomer, or you can save some money by learning to do this yourself. If you want to trim your pet's coat at home, you'll need to purchase an electric clipper made specifically for dogs. Typically, such clippers come with three combs: one with short teeth for clipping close to the skin around the head; a medium comb for the body; and a longer comb with wide teeth for the long hair on the legs. You'll also need a regular pet comb, hair-cutting scissors, and clipper oil.

Put your Cocker Spaniel on a table, so you don't have to bend over. Cover the table with an old sheet or tablecloth, which will catch most clipped fur. You may want to ask someone to help you hold your Cocker Spaniel still, and remember to bring several treats to reward him for good behavior.

Before starting, brush his hair carefully and remove any tangles and mats. Then, using the medium-sized comb, clip the hair on his back and upper sides. Move the clipper slowly, starting at his neck and working toward his tail. After this, switch to the longer comb and clip the fringe on the lower sides and his legs. You can use the scissors to trim the fringe, and to clip away hair on his paws. Then move to his chest, using the medium and long combs to ensure that his coat is shorter near the neck and longer at the lower part of his body.

The noise of the clipper will probably make your Cocker Spaniel uncomfortable at first, so it's best to wait until the end to trim his head. Use the short comb to clip his head and the fur on the tops of his ears, and use the scissors to trim the longer hairs at the ends of the ears. When you're finished clipping your Cocker Spaniel, give him a bath to wash away loose hairs and clipper oil.

Your first pet clips will probably look amateurish, but don't give up. This is something that will improve with practice, and your Cocker Spaniel's fur will grow back.

NAIL CARE: Nail care should be a part of your Cocker Spaniel's regular

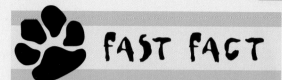

FAST FACT

If you are not prepared to dedicate the time and effort required to keep your Cocker Spaniel's coat looking its best, consider a short cut (known as a "pet trim" or "puppy cut") instead. This hairstyle will be much easier to brush and groom.

grooming routine. If nails are left to grow unchecked, they can cause discomfort. Overgrown nails can also lead to painful injuries for both dogs and people. Most Cocker Spaniels need to have their nails trimmed every three to four weeks.

Electric clippers can help to keep your Cocker Spaniel's coat looking its best.

There are several different types of tools that you can use to keep your Cocker Spaniel's nails properly trimmed.

Although a professional groomer or veterinarian can trim your dog's nails, this is something that can easily and inexpensively be done at home. To trim your dog's nails at home, you will need a pair of nail clippers that are specially made for dogs. It is also essential to have a styptic pencil, styptic powder, or another clotting agent on hand. If the nail is cut too short, it will bleed profusely until a clotting agent has been applied.

To avoid cutting the nail too short, search for the quick of the nail before trimming. The quick runs through the center of the nail. On dark or black nails, the quick is hard to see, but it must be avoided. If you can't see the quick, clip slowly and carefully. Trim off little bits at a time until you are sure of the quick's location.

Most dogs don't enjoy having their nails clipped. You can make the procedure more pleasant for everyone involved by getting your Cocker Spaniel used to nail care while he is still a puppy. Even before his nails are long enough to trim, touch his paws frequently, rubbing the nails gently with your fingers. This will get him used to having his nails touched. Showing him a pair of nail clippers every now and then at treat time won't hurt either.

When the nails are finally long enough to be trimmed, coax your puppy into a comfortable position. Hold him steady and begin cutting off the very ends of the nails. Be sure to speak to him in a soothing voice throughout the procedure so that he is put at ease. When you're finished, give him a treat and lots of praise.

EAR CARE: Cocker Spaniels are prone to ear infections and should have their ears cleaned at least twice each week. This is relatively easy to do at home. All you need are cotton balls and an ear cleaning solution, which can be purchased from a veterinarian or a pet supply store.

Squirt the recommended amount of cleaning solution into your dog's ears. Rub the outside of each ear gently in a downward motion to work the solution into all crevices. Then carefully use a cotton ball to clean dirt and wax from inside the ears.

Never stick your finger, a cotton swab, or anything else into your dog's ear canal. This will be uncomfortable for your pet, and could cause hearing damage. If your dog's ears are extremely dirty, bloody, or smelly, take him to the veterinarian immediately. There are some problems, including infection and ear mites, that cannot be resolved with a simple ear cleaner.

DENTAL CARE: Dental care should be part of a Cocker Spaniel's grooming routine. Like humans, dogs can suffer from tartar buildup, cavities, gum disease, and other dental issues. Periodontal disease can make it difficult for dogs to chew and may even be fatal if allowed to progress unchecked.

When your puppy is six months old, you should develop a biweekly brushing routine. Plaque will begin to develop on a puppy's permanent teeth at this age and should be removed periodically to avoid buildup. Brushing should be done

with a specially formulated doggie toothpaste and toothbrush. These items can be purchased from a pet supply store or veterinarian's office. You should never use human toothpaste to brush a Cocker Spaniel's teeth. Human toothpaste is harsh and may upset a dog's stomach.

Always brush your Cocker Spaniel's teeth gently using the amount of paste recommended on the tube. Make as many vertical passes with the brush as you can, lifting your dog's lips whenever necessary to reach the outer surface of each tooth. You can supplement brushing with chew toys and other products that are specifically designed to remove tartar buildup. These toys can be purchased from pet supply stores and may be available through your veterinarian's office.

When you take your Cocker Spaniel for his annual checkup, your vet will examine your pet's teeth and check for early signs of periodontal disease. If necessary, your vet can also clean and polish your Cocker Spaniel's teeth.

TRAINING YOUR COCKER SPANIEL

You must begin training your Cocker Spaniel as soon as you bring him home. He will need to be taught the household rules. He should be

Dogs need to learn good manners and basic household rules at an early age. If you don't want your Cocker Spaniel on the couch as an adult, don't let him sit there when he's a pup.

housebroken as soon as possible. And he should be taught to obey the basic commands that a well-behaved dog needs to know. Your Cocker Spaniel won't mind training sessions; in fact, he'll probably look forward to them. Dogs of this breed have high intelligence and a strong desire to please their owners, making them relatively easy to train.

You can probably do most of your dog's training at home. However, if you find that you are having difficul-

ty with the training process, contact a professional trainer for help. Professional trainers will be able to teach your Cocker Spaniel basic commands. They will also be able to teach you how to work with your pet.

Another option for pet owners is obedience school. Obedience schools are often less costly than professional trainers but they provide many of the same benefits. Owners are usually required to attend classes with their

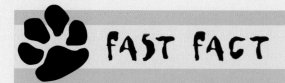

FAST FACT

Cocker Spaniels are motivated by treats. A few well-timed snacks during a training session can help encourage your pet to learn basic commands. Praise is also excellent motivation for the attention-loving Cocker Spaniel.

dogs. With the help of an instructor, you will learn how to teach basic commands, such as "sit," "down," "stay," "come," and "heel."

However you decide to train your Cocker Spaniel, it is important to remember that training is an ongoing process. Your pet will not be able to learn everything overnight. You must be patient and willing to work with him on a daily basis to mold him into a well-behaved dog.

HOUSEBREAKING

Housebreaking is one of the most difficult, yet most important, types of training. Like other dogs, Cocker Spaniels don't understand why they aren't allowed to relieve themselves in the house. It will be up to you to teach your pet that this behavior is unacceptable.

Cocker Spaniels can be trained either to relieve themselves outside, or to relieve themselves inside the house on paper. Outside is the preferred spot for most owners. Regardless of the spot you choose, you need to stick with it. Training a puppy to go outside and then switching to paper when it is convenient for you can be confusing for the puppy and may lead to lengthy setbacks.

It often takes at least six months for a puppy to gain control of his bladder and get into a proper routine. Until then, there will be lots and lots of accidents. But that's okay. Accidents are an inevitable part of raising and housebreaking a puppy. Cocker Spaniel puppies have very small bladders, so for their first few months it's physically impossible for them to hold urine for more than a few hours. Over time, they will gain more control. Until then, however, they will feel the need to eliminate every hour or two. Puppies will also want to go when they first wake up,

FAST FACT

Dogs are pack animals. This makes social order very important to them. If you establish yourself as pack leader though your behavior and body language, your Cocker Spaniel will acknowledge and respect your authority.

after they eat, and following playtime.

It is important to let your puppy outside during these times. Take him to his designated "potty area"; each time he goes to the bathroom there, praise him so that he knows you're pleased with his behavior.

If you are not able to let your puppy out as needed, you should consider hiring a pet sitter or dog walker to do it for you. Cocker Spaniels that are allowed to eliminate on the carpet and floor through part of the day do not understand why they cannot continue this behavior whenever it pleases them.

When your puppy does have an accident in the house, it is essential that you keep your cool. Getting angry or upset won't accomplish anything and in most cases will just make the situation worse. You should also avoid physical punishment. Spanking a dog—or worse, rubbing his nose in his own urine—will not teach him to go outside. It will, however, teach him that you are a cruel person who should not be trusted. Instead, clean up the mess as thoroughly as you can. Dogs like to eliminate in the same place again and again. Any scent that is left behind will encourage more accidents and bad behavior.

When housebreaking a puppy, technique is just as important as consistency. Many dog experts

Housetraining a Cocker Spaniel takes time and patience. When your dog does have an accident in the house, don't punish him. Instead, pick up or wipe up the mess with a paper towel, and take your dog and the mess outside. Place the mess in his designated potty area, then praise your dog as though he had gone in the right place. In time, he'll get the idea.

recommend using a crate to confine and housetrain a puppy. This may seem cruel but actually is not. Crates are easy for puppies to keep clean. They are small and den-like. Since dogs do not like to relieve themselves where they sleep, they will try to avoid going in their den for as long as possible.

If you don't want to crate your Cocker Spaniel, you can confine him to a small area of the house while you are away. A laundry room, kitchen, or another room that does not have carpet will work well for this purpose.

TEACHING BASIC COMMANDS

By the time he is six months old, every Cocker Spaniel should know the basic commands "sit," "down," "stay," "come," and "heel." Older dogs can be taught these commands, but they don't learn nearly as fast as puppies.

You can begin training your dog as soon as you bring him home, provided you keep the training sessions short and fun. Puppies have limited attention spans. They are easily distracted and will become bored if forced to participate in any one activity for too long.

It is usually easier to teach basic commands if you feed your puppy a treat when he does something right.

However, treats are not absolutely necessary. In many cases, praise will work just as well. Cocker Spaniels love to please their owners. If they receive lots of praise and petting for a specific behavior, they will often try to repeat that behavior in hopes of getting the same result.

SIT: This should be the first command you teach your Cocker Spaniel. After he masters sitting, you will find it easier not only to teach him other commands but also to control his behavior throughout the day. To begin, show your puppy that you have a treat in your hand. Hold the treat above your Cocker Spaniel's head and issue the "sit" command. The treat should be held high enough so that your puppy has to lift his nose up to get it, but not so high that jumping is required. The puppy should fall naturally into a sitting position to reach the treat. If he does not, you may apply very gentle pressure to his rear end (the area between the hip joints but below the spine). Praise your Cocker Spaniel enthusiastically and give him a bit of the treat as soon as he sits. Repeat the training exercise for two minutes straight, three or four times each day.

DOWN: You can begin teaching your Cocker Spaniel the "down" command as soon as he has learned how to sit. To start, get your Cocker Spaniel into a sitting position. Hold a treat in front of him at nose level. Then issue the "down" command. As you are speaking, lower the treat to ground level. Your treat-loving Cocker Spaniel should lean forward and follow the treat with his nose. As soon as his belly touches the ground, give him the treat along with a generous helping of praise. Repeat the exercise for two minutes straight, three or four times a day.

STAY/COME: Because the "stay" and "come" commands go hand in hand, you can teach these tricks simultaneously. Begin by getting your Cocker Spaniel to sit. If he is really antsy, you can tell him to lie down. Hold up your hand like a stop sign the second he is still. Give the "stay" command in a firm and confident voice. Don't expect the puppy to sit still for too long. Remember that he has no idea yet what "stay" means. If he does stay, even for a few seconds, give him lots of praise. Repeat this exercise a few times.

When your puppy seems to be getting the hang of it, start backing away slowly as you issue the "stay" command. Stop a step or two away from your puppy and issue the "come" command. You can use a treat to encourage him to come to you. Repeat the "stay" and "come" commands for at least two minutes straight, three or four times a day, gradually increasing the distance between you and your pet.

HEEL: A well-behaved dog will walk next to you, not pulling ahead on his leash. You can start teaching your dog to do this once he's mastered the "sit" command. Hook the leash to his collar, and get your Cocker Spaniel into a sitting position on your left side. As soon as you raise your foot to begin walking, issue the command "Heel" in a firm tone. If your dog runs ahead or lags behind, say "Heel" again. Keep him at your side the entire time, even when you turn. If you stop, your dog should sit at your side until you move and issue the "heel" command again.

Don't give your dog too much leash at first. This will reduce the need for you to tug on the lead and forcibly correct the dog. Also, be sure to praise your dog constantly when he follows the command. Offering occasional treats as a reward doesn't hurt either. Whatever you do, don't punish your Cocker Spaniel or jerk him around aggressively if he doesn't pick up on this skill right away. If you're patient and consistent, he will eventually learn.

CHAPTER SEVEN

Health Issues Your Cocker Spaniel May Face

Cocker Spaniels are a relatively healthy breed. But that doesn't mean you won't have to make an effort to keep your dog in good health. As the primary caregiver for your pet, it's up to you to make sure he gets the exercise, nutrition, and veterinary care he needs to live a long and healthy life.

Every Cocker Spaniel puppy needs an initial checkup. Your pet will also need to visit the vet regularly for vaccinations and wellness examinations. Cocker Spaniel puppies will also need a six-month exam and a one-year exam. After age one, Cocker Spaniels should be taken for a wellness exam at least once a year

Providing proper veterinary care is an important aspect of Cocker Spaniel ownership.

until they reach senior status, at about seven years. At that point, they will need a checkup every six months.

When conducting a wellness exam, the vet will check your Cocker Spaniel for any unusual lumps and bumps. Eyes, ears, teeth, and feet will be examined as well. Some vets also perform lab tests, such as urinalysis, heartworm checks, or blood panels, to verify the health of internal organs and systems.

Wellness exams are very important. They are the best way to evaluate your pet's general health. These exams can also make you and your vet aware of potential health problems before they become serious conditions or illnesses.

CHOOSING A VETERINARIAN

Selecting a veterinarian is an important decision. After all, you'll be entrusting the health care of your canine friend to that person, so you'll want to choose someone who is kind, competent, and knowledgeable. If you are a first-time pet owner, consider asking friends, family members, or neighbors who have a pet whether they can recommend a vet.

Finding a vet who is a member of the American Animal Hospital Association (AAHA) may also be a good idea. The AAHA is the only

Ideally, a prospective veterinary clinic should be a member of the American Animal Hospital Association or a similar organization that inspects and accredits veterinary facilities.

companion-animal veterinarian association in the United States. The organization has established high-quality standards for veterinarians and facilities. Vets who are members of the AAHA meet these standards. Their facilities are also inspected on a regular basis.

Another important factor to consider when choosing a veterinarian is the distance between your home and the vet's office. If your Cocker

Spaniel needs emergency medical care, the amount of time it takes you to get to a doctor could mean the difference between life and death.

Evaluating a vet's after-hours policy is also a must. Some vets handle after-hours emergencies themselves. Others use a calling service or refer patients to an animal hospital. If your Cocker Spaniel gets stung by a bee or eats something he shouldn't, it is reassuring to know that help is just a phone call away, no matter what time it is.

Before making any final choices, you should interview prospective vets and tour their facilities. Trust your judgment. If the staff seems unkind or if the facility looks dirty and unkempt, you will be much better off finding another vet.

WHAT TO EXPECT FROM YOUR FIRST VET VISIT

You should take your new Cocker Spaniel to the vet within 48 hours of picking him up from the breeder or shelter. The first trip to the vet will consist of a physical exam and a socialization checkup. Physical exams usually begin with a weigh-in and a temperature check. The vet will let you know whether your Cocker Spaniel is underweight or overweight, and advise you how to deal with such a problem.

The vet will then examine the puppy to make sure he is healthy, checking the puppy's ears, eyes, nose, mouth, and genitals before moving on to the skin and coat. Most vets will also listen to the puppy's heartbeat and check for parasites, hernias, and other health problems.

The vet should keep you updated throughout the exam, but you should not hesitate to ask any questions you might have. As a pet owner, it is your responsibility to know what is happening with your pet's health.

When the physical exam is complete, your vet will conduct a socialization checkup to make sure your puppy is developing properly. This will usually consist of a few simple tests. Afterward, the vet will be able to tell you if your puppy is submissive, dominant, independent,

FAST FACT

The initial vet visit is the perfect time to ask questions about training, exercise, nutrition, and other aspects of your Cocker Spaniel's care. The vet will be able to offer advice on all of these things and help you develop vaccination schedules, feeding schedules, and other important regimens to keep your pet healthy.

FAST FACT

When you take your purebred Cocker Spaniel puppy to the veterinarian for the first time, you should also take vaccination records, pedigree papers, and any other documents you received from the breeder.

or neutral. All of this information will be helpful when it comes time to housetrain and train your Cocker Spaniel.

Many vets will also want to conduct lab tests to check for parasites. This will require a fecal sample from your dog. You should take a fresh sample with you when you go. The sample can be placed in a plastic baggie or container and given to the veterinarian staff when you arrive.

VACCINATIONS

Your Cocker Spaniel puppy will need inoculations to protect him from serious and potentially fatal illnesses. Vaccinations will continue throughout the dog's life. Some vaccinations are optional, but most are required to keep your Cocker Spaniel in good health. Your veterinarian will be able to tell you which vaccinations your pet needs based on your location and lifestyle. Diseases and viruses your

Cocker Spaniel should be protected from include:

DISTEMPER: Distemper is a highly contagious disease related to measles. This dangerous virus can be transmitted through the air and through contact with urine, nasal secretions, and fecal matter. Virtually incurable, it is frequently fatal to small dogs like Cocker Spaniels. Infected dogs that do recover are almost always left paralyzed or partially paralyzed, and they often suffer irreparable damage to their nervous system and respiratory system.

Dogs that contract distemper will begin to exhibit symptoms of the disease within two weeks of being infected. Initial symptoms include vomiting, diarrhea, runny nose, weeping eyes, coughing, and a poor appetite. Puppies from three to six months old are especially vulnerable to distemper and must be vaccinated at the earliest opportunity.

HEPATITIS: Also known as canine adenovirus (CAV), infectious canine hepatitis is a contagious infection of the liver. Infected dogs, wolves, coyotes, bears, and other wildlife transmit the disease through feces, urine, blood, saliva, or eye and nasal discharge. The virus attacks the liver and the kidneys. It may cause bleeding disorders and, in extreme cases, death. Most healthy Cocker Spaniels can recover after a brief illness, but many are stricken with permanent kidney and liver conditions. Initial symptoms of canine hepatitis are fever, depression, coughing, poor appetite, vomiting, a tender

VACCINE SCHEDULE

According to the American Kennel Club (AKC), Cocker Spaniel puppies should receive their first inoculations at five to six weeks of age. However, veterinarians often have different vaccination protocols. Some vets follow the AKC recommendations; others prefer to wait until the puppy is at least eight weeks old. Regardless of individual protocol, your Cocker Spaniel should receive all inoculations required for the first year (besides a rabies shot) by the time he is 16 weeks old.

Here is a typical Cocker Spaniel vaccination schedule:

6 to 8 Weeks Old: First distemper, hepatitis, leptospirosis, parainfluenza, parvovirus shot. This is typically given in one combined injection known as the DHLPP shot or simply as the distemper shot.

10 to 12 Weeks Old: Second distemper, hepatitis, leptospirosis, parainfluenza, parvovirus (DHLPP) shot. Given in one combined injection.

14 to 16 Weeks Old: Third and final distemper, hepatitis, leptospirosis, parainfluenza, parvovirus (DHLPP) shot. Given in one combined injection.

3 to 6 Months Old: Rabies shot. Although this shot may be given to puppies as young as 12 weeks of age, some states will not recognize rabies vaccinations administered to puppies under 16 weeks old. Your veterinarian should be able to tell you more about the laws in your state.

Adult: Booster shots. After receiving initial inoculations, adult dogs need regular booster shots to protect against rabies, distemper, hepatitis, leptospirosis, parainfluenza, and parvovirus.

Your Cocker Spaniel may need additional vaccines for kennel cough, coronavirus, and Lyme disease depending on your lifestyle and location. Kennel cough and coronavirus vaccines can be administered after a Cocker Spaniel puppy is five weeks old. Lyme disease vaccinations can be started after 12 weeks of age and are usually given in two doses three weeks apart. All three vaccines require annual booster shots.

Core vaccinations that all dogs should receive include shots protecting against distemper, canine adenovirus, leptospirosis, para-influenza, parvovirus, and rabies. Follow your vet's recommendations with regard to the timing of your Cocker Spaniel's vaccinations.

abdomen, and diarrhea. Cocker Spaniel puppies are especially susceptible to this infection and should be vaccinated as soon as possible.

LEPTOSPIROSIS: Leptospirosis is a potentially fatal bacterial disease that is becoming more common worldwide. It damages the liver and kidneys of humans, cats, dogs, and other animals. Leptospirosis is most often carried in the urine of rats. Infected animals transmit the disease through blood or urine, which can contaminate soil and water. Recovered animals can also be carriers, and may continue to transmit the disease for months or even years.

Leptospirosis can lead to renal failure and death. The disease is treatable with penicillin if caught early enough. Dogs that do recover may suffer irreparable damage to their liver and kidneys.

The earliest symptoms of leptospirosis include fever, vomiting, diarrhea, poor appetite, stiffness, jaundice, internal bleeding, muscle pain, blood in the urine, depression, and lethargy. Some Cocker Spaniel puppies with leptospirosis will not exhibit any symptoms, which can make this disease difficult to catch in the early stages. For this reason, it is important to vaccinate your puppy as soon as possible.

PARAINFLUENZA: Parainfluenza is a highly contagious viral infection that causes respiratory problems. If left untreated, it can lead to pneumonia and death. Infected animals usually transmit the virus through nasal secretions. Initial symptoms of parainfluenza include fever, loss of appetite, and a dry, hacking cough.

PARVOVIRUS: Canine parvovirus, also known as parvo, is a highly contagious disease. There are two forms of this disease: cardiac and intestinal. Both can be transmitted from dog to dog through fecal matter. The virus can live for up to one year in the soil, and up to 10 days on feet, hair, and other objects.

Canine parvovirus is treatable if caught early, though even then the prognosis isn't great: half the dogs treated for parvovirus will die. Dogs that are not treated will die 90 percent of the time. Most deaths occur 24 to 72 hours after initial symptoms appear. Those symptoms include severe vomiting, bloody diarrhea, and a high fever.

All puppies are extremely susceptible to parvovirus, but small breeds such as Cocker Spaniels are more vulnerable than others. It is important to have your puppy vaccinated at the earliest opportunity. You should also keep your Cocker Spaniel away from other dogs and avoid walks in the park until his parvovirus inoculations are complete.

RABIES: Rabies is a viral disease that attacks the brain. Infected wildlife can transmit this disease to dogs through a bite and other forms of contact. Humans can also be infected with rabies. This disease is almost always fatal to dogs, and if untreated it is also fatal to humans. Animals that have contracted rabies will die within 10 days of being infected. Initial symptoms include fever, restlessness, aggressiveness, foaming at the mouth, lethargy, mania, and paralysis. Infected animals may also be sensitive to light. All states require dogs to be vaccinated for rabies. Your vet will be able to tell you how soon your Cocker Spaniel puppy can receive an inoculation for this deadly disease.

CORONAVIRUS: Canine coronavirus is a highly contagious virus that affects the intestinal tract of dogs. It can be transmitted through contact with fecal matter. The disease is not always life threatening, but it can cause a variety of health problems, including dehydration and respiratory issues. Puppies that have contracted coronavirus are more susceptible to parvovirus infection.

Complications can arise if an animal is infected with both at the same time. With the right medication, dogs can recover quickly. Most, however, will remain carriers of the disease for up to six months after recovery.

Initial symptoms of canine coronavirus include depression, fever, loss of appetite, vomiting, and diarrhea. Some vets will combine the coronavirus vaccine with vaccines for other diseases. Other vets consider the vaccine unnecessary. Your vet will be able to help you determine whether or not your Cocker Spaniel puppy needs to be inoculated against coronavirus.

KENNEL COUGH: Also known as tracheobronchitis, kennel cough is a highly contagious illness that affects the respiratory system of canines. The illness can be transmitted through the air, through contact with contaminated surfaces, or through direct contact. Kennel cough is manageable, but it can progress to pneumonia if left untreated. Pneumonia can be fatal in puppies and even in older dogs.

Symptoms of kennel cough typically begin three to five days after a dog has been infected. Initial symptoms include coughing, retching, sneezing, and vomiting. Some dogs will also become sensitive to light. A vaccine is recommended for Cocker Spaniels that spend time at the pet groomer, obedience school, kennel, and other places that contain multiple dogs.

LYME DISEASE: Lyme disease is an infectious bacterial illness that affects animals and humans. It is transmitted through the bite of an infected tick. Lyme disease can cause lameness, kidney problems, and other serious health issues. In rare cases, it can be fatal. Symptoms include lethargy, fever, muscle pain, vertigo, and neurological problems. The vaccine for Lyme disease can interfere with a dog's immune system. If you don't live in a high-risk area, your veterinarian may advise against this inoculation.

PARASITE CONTROL

Internal and external parasites, such as fleas, ticks, and worms, can cause serious medical problems for your Cocker Spaniel and for your family. To keep everyone in good health, you must do your best to prevent the following internal and external parasites:

FLEAS: Fleas are vicious little parasites. They clamp on to your Cocker Spaniel's hair and lay as many as 100 eggs on a daily basis. The eggs hatch

FAST FACT

Fleas often target specific areas on a dog, such as the neck, ears, abdomen, and base of the tail. To get rid of a flea infestation, you will need to treat both your pet and his environment.

quickly, which means it won't take long for your pet and your home to become completely infested. Some dogs are allergic to flea saliva and suffer terrible reactions when bitten. Severe flea problems can also lead to hair loss, anemia, and various illnesses. Flea infestations are a nightmare to eliminate. Fortunately, products such as flea collars can prevent infestations.

TICKS: Ticks are often found in hot and humid areas. They are not as common as fleas, but they can wreak just as much havoc. Ticks can transmit several different diseases to dogs, including Lyme disease and spotted fever. These parasites are generally controlled and prevented the same way fleas are. Your Cocker Spaniel can also be vaccinated for Lyme disease for extra protection.

If you see a tick on your dog, remove it immediately. Using tweezers, grab the tick as close to your Cocker Spaniel's skin as possible and pull straight out, using steady pressure. If you yank the tick out, the head may remain embedded in the skin, and can become infected. After the tick has been removed, apply antiseptic ointment to the bite area.

After outdoor play, always check your Cocker Spaniel for ticks. Remove these tiny parasites promptly, as they can cause your pet to become very sick.

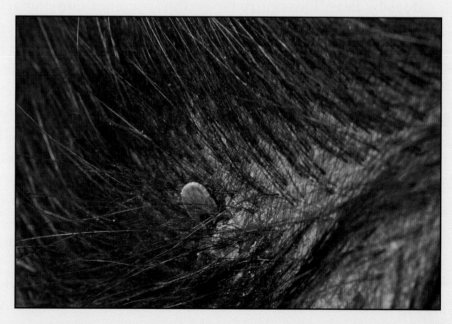

MITES: Mites, like fleas and ticks, are external parasites. There are six types of mites that attack dogs. All cause some form of mange. Certain types of mange, such as sarcoptic mange (scabies), are extremely contagious and can be passed to other animals as well as to humans. In nearly every case, your Cocker Spaniel will itch like crazy. Hair loss, dandruff, and dry skin may also occur. The most severe mite infestations can cause serious medical problems. If caught early on, however, every form of mange is treatable by a veterinarian.

TAPEWORMS: Various species of tapeworm can come from uncooked meat and fish, but these internal parasites are usually transmitted to dogs by fleas. Fleas carry tapeworm larvae, and transmit it to your dog when he eats an infested flea.

Tapeworms aren't usually life threatening to dogs; however, they can cause liver disease and other medical problems. If your Cocker Spaniel begins losing weight, or if you see evidence of tapeworm in his stool, you should contact your vet immediately for the appropriate worm medication. You should also treat both your dog and home for fleas to prevent the return of tapeworms.

HEARTWORMS: Heartworms are very common in many areas of the country and can be transmitted to your dog by infected mosquitoes. These internal parasites set up shop in your dog's heart and lungs. If your pet is affected by heartworms, he may appear weak, lose weight, or have a serious cough. Left untreated, heartworms can cause death. There are ways to prevent heartworms, but the preventive medicines can compromise a Cocker Spaniel's immune system. Talk to your vet to determine whether or not you should give your pet preventive medication.

ROUNDWORMS: Roundworms are internal parasites commonly transmitted from mother to puppy, but they can also be contracted if a dog comes into contact with soil or feces that has been infested with eggs. Roundworms can be fatal to puppies and may cause serious problems in adult dogs. They can infect people too. No preventive medicines are 100 percent effective against roundworms, so you should get your Cocker Spaniel tested on an annual basis. If you notice any spaghetti-like worms in your pet's feces, contact your vet right away.

HOOKWORMS: Like roundworms, hookworms are internal parasites that can be transferred from mother to puppy and through exposure to contaminated soil or feces. Hookworms can cause serious anemia and diarrhea and are dangerous to both dogs and humans. Symptoms of a hookworm infestation include dark stool, weight loss, skin problems, and weakness. Your veterinarian can easily treat hookworm and may be able to provide you with a preventive medication.

WHIPWORMS: Whipworms are considered the worst of all internal parasites because they are so hard to detect and so difficult to treat. The only way for a vet to determine that your Cocker Spaniel is infested with whipworms is by examining the dog's fecal matter, a method that is not always foolproof. Whipworms are acquired from contaminated soil or feces. These nasty parasites can cause colic, stomach pain, diarrhea, and weight loss. Treatment is tricky, but available.

——————

Parasites are much easier to prevent than they are to eradicate. Your vet will be able to offer you information on the various types of preventive medicine available. The vet can also test your Cocker Spaniel annually to make sure there are no unseen problems.

BREED-SPECIFIC HEALTH PROBLEMS

Cocker Spaniels are a relatively healthy breed. However, no breed is entirely free of hereditary problems, and Cocker Spaniels are genetically predisposed to a number of health conditions. In particular, Cocker Spaniels are highly susceptible to inherited eye problems. Other health issues include allergies, epilepsy, hip dysplasia, hypothyroidism, intervertebral disc disease, patellar luxation, phosphofruktokinase deficiency, and seborrhea.

ALLERGIES: Many dogs, including Cocker Spaniels, suffer from pollen or food allergies. Pollen allergies are typically seasonal, but food allergies can make a dog suffer year-round. Most Cocker Spaniels react to allergies by scratching, licking, or biting themselves. Determining exactly what a dog is allergic to can be difficult and may take some time, but it is possible to figure out whether the problem is being caused by an airborne allergy, a food ingredient, or something else. Treatment for allergies may include antihistamines, glucocorticoids, or a hypoallergenic diet.

CATARACTS: Cataracts are among the most common eye problems that affect Cocker Spaniels. The issue occurs when the lens of the eye becomes cloudy and impairs vision. Cataracts are frequently inherited, but can also be caused by an injury to the eye or the onset of diabetes. The condition is visibly noticeable and easily diagnosed. Although cataracts are not painful, they can cause impairment of vision or blindness. Fortunately, with surgery cataracts can almost always be removed.

Selecting a Cocker Spaniel from dogs that have been free of eye diseases for at least two generations is the best way to ensure your pet will not suffer from hereditary eye problems. The Canine Eye Registration Foundation and the American Spaniel Club both maintain a registry of dogs that have been certified as unaffected by certain hereditary eye diseases.

CHERRY EYE: Also known as canine nictitans gland prolapse, cherry eye occurs when a tear gland in the eyelid swells and protrudes from the edge of the lid. The condition isn't painful, but it isn't very attractive either. The protruding gland appears as a round red mass that looks rather like a tumor. Cherry eye can usually be corrected with surgery. The gland is not removed; instead, it is repositioned so that the Cocker Spaniel does not suffer from another condition, dry-eye syndrome, throughout the rest of his life. This procedure may need to be repeated after some time has passed. Cherry eye is most common in Cocker Spaniel puppies, but it can affect older dogs as well.

DRY-EYE SYNDROME: Dry-eye syndrome, also known as kerato-conjunctivitis sicca (KCS), occurs when a dog cannot create enough tears. Cocker Spaniels are affected by this condition more than any other breed. Dry-eye syndrome can be painful because it causes the cornea, or outer part of the eye, to dry out. Symptoms include reddened or dull eyes, frequent blinking, and a thick discharge of greenish or yellowish mucus. A veterinarian can typically diagnose dry-eye syndrome with a simple and inexpensive test. The condition can then be treated appropriately. Cocker Spaniels with mild cases can be given artificial tear solutions that are available over the counter. More severe cases can be treated with drug therapy or a surgical procedure that reroutes salivary ducts to the eye.

EPILEPSY: Epilepsy is a disorder of the nervous system that is fairly common among Cocker Spaniels. Dogs who suffer from epilepsy have seizures that can vary in intensity. A petit mal seizure may cause a dog to stare into space, salivate, or tremble. A grand mal seizure is more serious; the dog may fall to the ground, clamp his jaws, shake uncontrollably, or paddle his legs. A veterinarian should examine any dog that suffers either type of seizure. Seizures may be the result of idiopathic epilepsy, the cause of which is not known, or a sign of another illness, such as cancer or liver disease. If another illness is not present, epileptic seizures can typically be managed with medication, exercise, acupuncture, or a combination of all three treatments.

GLAUCOMA: Glaucoma is a painful eye condition that occurs when pressure builds in the eyeball. The condition is usually genetic, but can also be the result of an injury or another eye condition. If left untreated, glaucoma can destroy a Cocker Spaniel's retina and cause blindness within hours. Symptoms include an enlarged eyeball, redness of the eye, loss of vision, and lethargy. Glaucoma is usually treated with medication or a surgical procedure.

HIP DYSPLASIA: Many breeds have a genetic tendency toward hip dysplasia, and Cocker Spaniels are no exception. This potentially crippling condition is the result of an abnormality in the development of the hip joint. Hip dysplasia does not normally become evident until a Cocker Spaniel is between six and eight months old. Although it is a genetic problem, environmental factors can impact the severity of the condition. Dogs that jump a lot or are overweight, for example, may suffer more pain or faster deterioration of the joint.

Initial symptoms of hip dysplasia include difficulty walking or jumping. As the condition progresses, dogs tend to lose muscle strength and may need help standing. Treatment is possible, although it often depends on the dog's age and the extent of the problem. Common treatments include medication, weight management, periods of rest, surgery, and full hip replacements.

HYPOTHYROIDISM: Hypothyroidism is a hormonal disorder that affects many different breeds, but it is especially prevalent among Cocker Spaniels. The condition, which is considered hereditary, is caused by low levels of thyroid hormones. Symptoms include dry skin, hair loss, chronic ear infection, weight gain, lethargy, and depression.

Hypothyroidism cannot be cured, but it can be treated with medication. Cocker Spaniels that suffer from this disorder usually need medicine for the rest of their lives to remain symptom-free.

INTERVERTEBRAL DISC DISEASE (IVDD): Also known as "slipped disc disease," IVDD is a spinal condition that frequently affects breeds with long backs or short legs. This debilitating disease occurs when a disk bulges or ruptures and slips in the middle of the back. The first signs of IVDD are weakness, a stiff gait, and lack of coordination. Paralysis can also occur in the most severe cases.

Cocker Spaniels that suffer from IVDD almost always need prolonged cage rest and surgery to correct the disc. If the dog has some sensation in his hind legs prior to surgery, it is highly likely that he will regain his ability to walk after successful surgery and rehabilitative care.

PATELLAR LUXATION: Patellar luxation is a congenital anomaly commonly seen in small breeds like Cocker Spaniels. This condition occurs when the kneecap, or patella, slips out of position and rides on the inside or outside of its normal groove. Patellar luxation is usually apparent by the time a dog is six months old. Initial symptoms can include pain and a hitch in the gait. Dogs may also extend their leg in an attempt to get the kneecap to pop back into place.

Patellar luxation can grow progressively worse. Treatment varies, depending on the severity of the condition, but the most common treatment is surgery. The prognosis is usually very good for dogs that are treated early.

PHOSPHOFRUCTOKINASE DEFICIENCY (PFK): This genetic disease affects approximately 1 percent of Cocker Spaniels. The condition interferes with the formation of red blood cells and the conversion of glucose to energy. Common symptoms include fever, depression, anemia, lethargy, muscle cramping, and intolerance to exercise. Dogs with PFK can usually lead a relatively normal life if they avoid strenuous exercise and stressful environments. A bone marrow transplant can also bring relief, but this procedure can be very expensive and requires a healthy donor.

PROGRESSIVE RETINAL ATROPHY (PRA): Progressive retinal atrophy is an inherited eye condition that is most commonly seen in Cocker Spaniels between three and six years old. The condition occurs when the retina begins to deteriorate. It is a progressive disease that cannot be treated and will eventually lead to blindness. Early symptoms of PRA include vision impairment at night or in low-light situations. Further symptoms include dilated pupils, hyper-reflectivity, and complete loss of sight.

RETINAL DYSPLASIA: Retinal dysplasia is an eye problem that can affect Cocker Spaniel puppies. The condition occurs when layers of the retina fold during development. A mild case of retinal dysplasia will not affect vision, but a more severe case can cause one or more blind spots on the eye. Retinal dysplasia is almost always inherited but can also be a result of a parvovirus infection or from trauma to the eye. The condition can be diagnosed with an eye exam, but is not treatable.

SEBORRHEA: Seborrhea is a skin dis-

FAST FACT

Although it is not common, some Cocker Spaniels suffer from congenital deafness. This condition can make training and communicating more difficult, but most dogs will still be able to function and live well with a hearing disability.

order common among Cocker Spaniels. The condition occurs when the epidermis, or outer layer of skin, and the sebaceous glands produce excessive scale and sebum. Symptoms include itching, dry flakes in the hair, and greasy skin. Seborrhea usually appears in dogs that are less than two years old, but it has been known to affect older Cocker Spaniels as well.

Diagnosis typically requires a skin biopsy, though an experienced veterinarian may be able to recognize the condition by conducting a visual examination. Cases can range from mild to severe. The most severe form of Seborrhea can result in recurring bacteria and yeast infections. Seborrhea can usually be managed with medicated shampoos and moisturizers. Drug therapy is also available.

CHAPTER EIGHT

Enjoying and Caring for Your Adult Cocker Spaniel

Caring for an adult Cocker Spaniel is a lot like caring for a puppy. As an adult, your Cocker Spaniel will still need plenty of love, attention, and guidance. The difference is that you will probably have more time to devote to these things now that your dog is housebroken and able to follow basic commands.

You can use this extra time to have fun and enjoy each other's company. Together, you can take walks, hunt, and participate in other activities. You may want to get your Cocker Spaniel involved in competitive activities, such as conformation shows, agility contests, or tracking tests. Just about anything you want to do will be fine with

Your Cocker Spaniel will be happiest when you are spending time with him.

your Cocker Spaniel, as long as you're doing it together.

ADVANCED TRAINING

The term *advanced training* usually refers to anything beyond basic obedience training. Cocker Spaniels can be taught to walk properly off a leash, catch and retrieve objects, and do many other types of things.

Like regular obedience training, advanced training takes time and dedication. No one skill is easier to teach than another, but different approaches can be used during the training process. You can train your Cocker Spaniel at home or make use of professional courses or handlers.

The following paragraphs offer a brief summary of training methods that can be used to teach your Cocker Spaniel how to walk off a leash and how to catch and retrieve. These skills will come in handy if you want your pet to compete in dog shows, participate in competitive sports like flyball, or serve as a hunting companion. Since no one method

If you're looking for an alternative form of exercise for your pet, consider swimming. Most Cocker Spaniels love to swim, and as a breed these dogs tend to be adept in the water.

is right for every dog, feel free to adjust these techniques to suit your Cocker Spaniel.

WALKING OFF A LEASH: Training a dog to walk off a leash is a lot like training a dog to walk on a leash properly, as discussed on page 72. You use the same commands ("sit" and "heel"); you just don't use a leash. This trick is best taught when your Cocker Spaniel has completely mastered walking on a leash.

To start, position the dog on your left side and tell him to sit. When you begin walking, give the "heel" command. If your dog does not stay at your side and maintain your walking pace, give the "heel" command again. Praise him when he does this correctly. When you stop, command him to "sit."

If your Cocker Spaniel cannot behave or follow your every command, then he is probably not ready to walk off a leash quite yet. You may also want to make sure you conduct training in a fenced-in yard or enclosed area. You don't want your unleashed Cocker Spaniel to run off in pursuit of a bird, rabbit, or other distraction.

CATCH AND RETRIEVE: Teaching your Cocker Spaniel to catch and retrieve can be fun for both you and your pet. This activity is great exercise for dogs. It also provides an

This English Cocker Spaniel has been taught to catch a ball and return it to his owner.

opportunity for you and your Cocker Spaniel to bond with one another.

To get a dog to catch or retrieve anything, you must first get him interested in the object. For example, if you want to teach him to catch and retrieve a ball, then you should get him to want to touch the ball. As soon as your Cocker Spaniel takes the ball (or Frisbee, or whatever else you are using), give him lots of praise so that he knows you approve.

The next step is getting him to chase the ball when you throw it. Start with low, short throws that are easy for him to follow. If you want him to retrieve the ball and bring it back to you, give him a command like "fetch" or "retrieve." Then, coax him into bringing the ball back by calling his name or giving the "come" command. If necessary, use a treat as extra encouragement.

If you want him to catch the ball, throw it gently into the air in his direction while issuing the command "catch." Be sure to use a soft ball so that your Cocker Spaniel won't be hurt if he misses and the ball hits him in the face.

COMPETITIONS FOR COCKER SPANIELS

Many different competitive events are open to purebred Cocker Spaniels. The American Kennel Club sanctions some events; breed clubs, such as the American Spaniel Club or the English Cocker Spaniel Club of America, sponsor other competitions. These events give you a chance to show off your pet's skills and personality. Some of the most popular competitions for Cocker Spaniels include conformation shows, obedience trials, agility trials, and tracking tests.

CONFORMATION SHOWS: There are three basic types of conformation shows: all-breed, specialty, and group. All-breed shows—the type most frequently seen on television—give dogs in any of the more than 150 AKC-recognized breeds a chance to shine. Specialty shows are open to dogs of a specific breed. For example, the American Spaniel Club holds a specialty show that is just for American Cocker Spaniels. Group shows are for dogs of one group, such as the sporting group. The AKC includes both American and English Cocker Spaniels in this group, along with other spaniels and dogs like the Golden Retriever, the Irish Setter, and the Labrador Retriever.

Dogs don't necessarily compete against one another in any of these conformation shows. Instead, they are judged against the standard for their breed. The dog that comes closest to the breed standard usually wins the competition. However, a dog with exceptional personality and showmanship can receive extra points, tipping the scales in his favor.

To be eligible for participation in a conformation show, Cocker Spaniels must be at least six months old and AKC registered. Male and female Cocker Spaniels compete separately in one of six classes: puppy (for dogs less than one year old); 12–18 months; novice (for dogs that are not first-prize winners); amateur-owner-handler (for dogs that are not champions and owners who have never worked as a professional handler); American-bred (for dogs born and bred in the United States); and open (for all dogs over six months old).

OBEDIENCE TRIALS: Obedience trials focus on a Cocker Spaniel's skills, rather than his appearance. Competitions can be found for dogs of all skill levels. Special titles or ribbons may be awarded in AKC-sponsored obedience trials. To participate, a Cocker Spaniel must be at least six months old. They must also be able to follow basic commands.

The skills required vary, depending on the level of competition. Dogs at the novice level are often asked to stand for examination, walk on and off a leash, sit, lie down, come when called, and navigate various obstacles. At the advanced level, dogs may be expected to obey nonverbal commands or distinguish a handler's scent from among a pile of items.

AGILITY TRIALS: Like obedience trials, agility trials focus on a dog's skills. In agility trials, dogs race through an obstacle course with guidance from their owners or handlers. Courses usually include jumps, weave poles, pipe tunnels, and dog walks. Cocker Spaniels can earn many different titles and are eligible to participate in classes of varying skill levels. To take part in an AKC-sanctioned agility event, dogs must be at least one year old.

TRACKING TESTS: Because of their excellent sense of smell, Cocker Spaniels tend to do very well in

FAST FACT

Cocker Spaniels can participate in AKC Rally competitions. These competitions are a lot like obedience trials. A Rally competition requires dogs and their handlers to work together to complete a course of obedience exercises.

Cocker Spaniels are good athletes and can succeed in agility and rally competitions.

tracking tests. The AKC administers tracking tests at three different levels and holds a national invitational every year. The three tracking titles that can be earned include Tracking Dog (for following a 440-to-500-yard track with several turns), Tracking Dog Excellent (for following a 1,000-yard track with several turns), and Variable Surface Tracking (for following a scent over three different surfaces on an 800-yard track).

HUNTING WITH COCKER SPANIELS

Cocker Spaniels were originally bred to hunt. If you enjoy this activity, your pet may make a perfect hunting companion. A trained Cocker Spaniel can find, flush, and retrieve game. They are also able to competently track any animal that is on the run.

If you are interested in hunting with your Cocker Spaniel, you can begin training him for this sport as soon he's mastered the basic

Both American and English Cocker Spaniels can be trained as gun dogs, working with their hunter masters to flush and retrieve partridges and other small game birds.

obedience commands and has learned how to walk off a leash and retrieve an object. When you begin working in the field, it's a good idea to let him watch an older Cocker Spaniel that has been trained for tracking and hunting. This will give your dog a better idea of what flushing and retrieving game is all about. With hard work and patience, a Cocker Spaniel can be ready to hunt in less than a year.

TRAVELING WITH YOUR COCKER SPANIEL

If you like to travel, your Cocker Spaniel will probably be glad to join you on trips and vacations. As long as he can handle car rides or air travel, there is no reason why he can't come along. Before taking your Cocker Spaniel anywhere, make sure that he has proper identification. If you'll be vacationing far from home, have a special ID tag made that includes your local phone number or a cell phone number. This way you can be reached if your pet wanders off and gets lost. You will also want to take everything you'll need to care for him, including a collar, leash, medications, toys, food, treats, and dishes.

When traveling by car, make sure that your dog is securely fastened, either with a dog seatbelt harness, in his crate, or behind a vehicle barrier. Make sure to schedule regular stops

FAST FACT

During the hours before traveling, don't let your Cocker Spaniel eat or drink much. A long plane or car ride can be an especially upsetting experience for a dog that has had too much food or water.

where your Cocker Spaniel can stretch, sniff around, and go to the bathroom.

Flying with your Cocker Spaniel will require some preparation on your part. Every airline has different policies when it comes to canine passengers. Some airlines will allow you to take a small dog with you in the plane's cabin, so long as he's in a plastic crate. Others make dogs ride in an area that is separate from human passengers. The airline may have special guidelines about the size of your dog's crate. It may also require you to provide copies of paperwork showing that he is properly licensed and up-to-date on his vaccinations. Check with the airline you'll be using before it is time to leave so that you don't have any last-minute problems or expenses.

CANINE GOOD CITIZEN TEST

In 1989, the American Kennel Club started a new program known as the Canine Good Citizen (CGC) Program. Its goal is to promote well-mannered dogs and responsible pet ownership. Dogs that pass the 10-step obedience test are awarded a certificate from the AKC.

The Canine Good Citizen Test is a pass/fail test. To earn a certificate, Cocker Spaniels must prove that they can accept a friendly stranger, sit and stay on command, sit politely for petting, stand for grooming and examination, walk on a leash, walk through a crowd, come when called, react appropriately to other dogs, stay calm when distracted, and behave when left alone with a friendly stranger for at least three minutes. More information is available online at http://www.akc.org/events/cgc.

Dogs of any breed or age are eligible to participate in the test, which is typically administered by dog clubs, community organizations, 4-H groups, and veterinary associations. Participating in the CGC Program is a good way to reward your dog for having good manners. It also provides a good foundation for participation in other events, such as conformation shows and obedience trials.

For Cocker Spaniel owners who live in England, Northern Ireland, Scotland, or Wales, the Kennel Club of the United Kingdom runs a similar training program called the Good Citizen Dog Scheme. Information about this program can be found online at http://www.thekennel-club.org.uk/dogtraining.

If you're taking a Cocker Spaniel on the road, he should be restrained for safety. You could put him in a pet carrier or purchase a special harness that attaches to the seat belts.

When traveling, plan your overnight accommodations in advance. Not all hotels or motels will accept pets. Hotels and resorts that accommodate dog owners can be found online at PetsWelcome.com, PetTravel.com, LetsGoPets.com, and other Web sites.

TRAVELING WITHOUT YOUR COCKER SPANIEL

If you must leave town and can't take your Cocker Spaniel along, you'll need to make arrangements for his care. A friend or family member might be able to look after your dog. If not, you could hire a professional pet sitter to watch your Cocker Spaniel. Before doing this, it's always a good idea to get recommendations and interview candidates.

Other options include boarding kennels and doggie day care centers. These facilities will care for your dog, exercise him, groom him, and play with him while you are away.

The best facilities have a veterinarian on staff to help with medical problems.

You can find boarding kennels and doggie day care centers in your area by using the phone book or the Internet. Your veterinarian as well as pet-owning family members and friends might also be able to give you recommendations. After finding a suitable option, you might want to tour the facility to see where your pet will be staying. The kennel or center you choose should be clean, safe, and large enough to accommodate your pet. There should also be separate areas for animals that are sick or aggressive. If the facility does not measure up to your standards, trust your instincts and look for another boarding option for your pet.

CARING FOR YOUR SENIOR PET

Cocker Spaniels are usually considered seniors after seven years. When your pet reaches this age, you may begin noticing changes in his physical appearance and temperament. Gray hair will appear around his face, paws, and other areas. His eating, playing, and sleeping habits may also change. For the first time since he was a puppy, your Cocker Spaniel may begin to have house-soiling accidents. Barking, whining, and

destructive behavior may also occur when your pet is upset or left home alone.

These changes can be painful to watch, but they don't have to diminish your pet's quality of life. If you are patient, loving, and understanding, you can make the aging process easier on him. Consistent affection and treatment will help him grow old with dignity.

NUTRITION

The right diet can also make things easier on a senior Cocker Spaniel. Older dogs have a different lifestyle than younger dogs. They also have different nutritional needs. Senior dogs need food that is easy to chew and digest. Small kibble is usually best, providing your dog has healthy teeth and the ability to chew kibble.

Like other dogs, senior dogs should eat a combination of protein, carbohydrates, and fiber. However,

FAST FACT

Older Cocker Spaniels may develop lumps and bumps on their body. Often these are benign, but you should always check with your veterinarian to make sure new growths are nothing to worry about.

You may notice that your senior Cocker Spaniel is slowing down with age, but he'll still enjoy talking walks and spending time with you.

their food should be low in fat. A light protein such as lamb, mixed with a carbohydrate like rice, works well for most senior dogs. If possible, you should steer clear of dog foods that contain red dye. Some senior Cocker Spaniels have allergic reactions to this unnecessary additive.

In addition to different food, you'll probably have to consider different portion sizes. As dogs age, their metabolism changes. Many older dogs also sleep more and exercise less. They don't need as much food as they did when they were young. Controlling the amount your Cocker Spaniel eats will prevent unhealthy weight gain. You can determine the best portion size for your dog by speaking to your veterinarian.

HEALTH PROBLEMS

Taking your Cocker Spaniel to the vet regularly—every six months once he turns seven—and making sure that he eats properly will help him have a longer, healthier life. But no matter how well you care for your Cocker Spaniel, certain age-related health problems cannot be prevented. Some can be treated and managed if diagnosed early enough. If your senior Cocker Spaniel develops one of the following conditions, your veterinarian will be able to provide

information and discuss treatment options to help your senior pet enjoy the best quality of life possible.

COGNITIVE DYSFUNCTION SYNDROME: Known more commonly as "old-dog syndrome," cognitive dysfunction syndrome (CDS) is the progressive deterioration of cognitive abilities. In plain English, this means your Cocker Spaniel is slowing down mentally. Common signs of CDS include sleeping more during the day, frequent potty accidents, confusion or forgetfulness, and a decreased desire to socialize. More than half of all senior dogs exhibit some level of CDS. Treatments include medication and therapy.

HEARING AND VISION LOSS: It is not uncommon for older dogs to suffer from progressive hearing or vision loss. Hearing problems are generally caused by deterioration of the ear. Vision loss can result from cataracts or other age-related issues. Treatment may or may not be available for both, depending on the specific problem.

HEART DISEASE: Older Cocker Spaniels, like humans, can suffer from heart disease. Some of the early symptoms include coughing and labored breathing. Your vet can

Looking at photos of you and your beloved Cocker Spaniel taken during happy times can help ease the pain of his passing.

check for cardiac problems when performing a physical. The vet will also be able to advise you about the various treatment options that are available.

ARTHRITIS: Many senior Cocker Spaniels suffer from arthritis, an extremely painful and degenerative joint disease. Symptoms can be hard to spot at first. But as the disease becomes progressively worse, your pet will move with obvious stiffness. He will also have difficulty jumping on furniture or climbing stairs. He may even become aggressive when the pain becomes unbearable. There is no way to cure arthritis. However, your vet will be able to help you develop a treatment plan to manage the condition with a combination of medicine, supplements, and exercise therapy.

SAYING GOOD-BYE

Saying good-bye to your beloved Cocker Spaniel can be difficult, but it is an inevitable part of pet ownership. If your dog is lucky, he will die peacefully in his sleep at a ripe old age. If not, it will be up to you to make difficult decisions about your pet's life and death.

Your veterinarian can help you determine whether or not your dog is past the point of curing or treatment. Although it can be difficult to face the possibility of euthanasia, you do not want your pet to suffer extreme pain or discomfort.

Euthanasia is the planned killing of a dog by means of injection. Other than the initial poke from the needle, the procedure is painless for the dog. It will, however, be very painful for you. It is terrible being

FAST FACT

Many veterinarians offer cremation services. Private crematoriums and pet cemeteries can also be located through the International Association of Pet Cemeteries Web site, www.iaopc.com.

forced to put a precious pet to sleep. At the same time, it may be the kindest thing you can do for a Cocker Spaniel that is suffering and unable to enjoy the simple pleasures of life.

No matter how your Cocker Spaniel dies, allow yourself time to grieve. If you need help with the process, there are many national and local support groups. Sharing your experience and stories about your pet may help you cope with the situation. With time, perhaps, you may feel ready to find another pet. Maybe you'll even decide that you'd like to bring another Cocker Spaniel into your life!

Organizations to Contact

American Animal Hospital Association
12575 West Bayaud Ave.
Lakewood, CO 80228
Phone: 303-986-2800
Fax: 800-252-2242
E-mail: info@aahanet.org
Web site: www.aahanet.org

American Canine Association, Inc.
P.O. Box 808
Phoenixville, PA 19460
Phone: 800-651-8332
Fax: 800-422-1864
E-mail: acacanines@aol.com
Web site: www.acainfo.com

American Dog Breeders Assn.
P.O. Box 1771
Salt Lake City, UT 84110
Phone: 801-936-7513
E-mail: bstofshw@adba.cc
Web site: www.adbadogs.com

American Humane Association
63 Inverness Dr. East
Englewood, CO 80112
Phone: 303-792-9900
Fax: 303-792-5333
Web site: www.americanhumane.org

American Kennel Club
8051 Arco Corporate Dr., Suite 100
Raleigh, NC 27617
Phone: 919-233-9767
E-mail: info@akc.org
Web site: www.akc.org

American Spaniel Club Inc.
P. O. Box 4194
Frankfort, KY 40604
Phone: 502-875-4489
Fax: 866-243-1068
E-mail: ASC.Secretary@gmail.com
Web site: www.asc-cockerspaniel.org

Association of Pet Dog Trainers
150 Executive Center Dr., Box 35
Greenville, SC 29615
Phone: 800-738-3647
E-mail: information@apdt.com
Web site: www.apdt.com

The Canadian Kennel Club
89 Skyway Avenue, Suite 100
Etobicoke, Ontario, M9W 6R4
Canada
Phone: 416-675-5511
Fax: 416-675-6506
E-mail: information@ckc.ca
Web site: www.ckc.ca/en

**Canine Eye Registration
Foundation**
1717 Philo Road
P.O. Box 3007
Urbana, IL 61803-3007
Phone: 217-693-4800
Fax: 217-693-4801
E-mail: cerf@vmdb.org
Web site: www.vmdb.org/cerf.html

**Canine Health
Foundation**
P.O. Box 37941
Raleigh, NC 27627-7941
Phone: 888-682-9696
Fax: 919-334-4011
E-mail: akcchf@akc.org
Web site: www.akcchf.org

Delta Society
875 124th Ave., NE
Suite 101
Bellevue, WA 98005
Phone: 425-226-7357
E-mail: info@deltasociety.org
Web site: www.deltasociety.org

**English Cocker Spaniel
Club of America Inc.**
P.O. Box 252
Hales Corners, WI 53130
Phone: 414-529-9714
E-mail: ecsca@ecsca.org
Web site: www.ecsca.org

**Humane Society
of the United States**
2100 L St., NW
Washington, DC 20037
Phone: 202-452-1100
Fax: 301-548-7701
E-mail: info@hsus.org
Web site: www.hsus.org

**The Kennel Club
of the United Kingdom**
1-5 Clarges St.
Picadilly, London W1J 8AB
United Kingdom
Phone: 0870 606 6750
Fax: 020 7518 1058
Web site: www.thekennelclub.org.uk

**National Association of Dog
Obedience Instructors**
PMB 369
729 Grapevine Hwy
Hurst, TX 76054-2085
E-mail: corrsec2@nadoi.org
Web site: www.nadoi.org

**National Association of
Professional Pet Sitters (NAPPS)**
17000 Commerce Parkway, Suite C
Mt. Laurel, NJ 08054
Phone: 856-439-0324
Fax: 856-439-0525
E-mail: napps@ahint.com
Web site: www.petsitters.org

National Dog Registry
P.O. Box 51105
Mesa, AZ 85208
Phone: 800-NDR-DOGS
E-mail: info@nationaldogregistry.com
Web site: www.nationaldogregistry.com

**North American Dog Agility
Council (NADAC)**
P.O. Box 1206
Colbert, OK 74733
E-mail: info@nadac.com
Web site: www.nadac.com

**North American Flyball
Association (NAFA)**
1400 West Devon Ave., #512
Chicago, IL 60660
Phone: 800-318-6312
E-mail: flyball@flyball.org
Web site: www.flyball.org

**North American Versatile
Hunting Dog Association**
P.O. Box 520
Arlington Heights, IL 60006
Phone: 847-253-6488
Fax: 847-255-5987
E-mail: navoffice@navhda.org
Web site: www.navhda.org

**Orthopedic Foundation
for Animals (OFA)**
2300 East Nifong Boulevard
Columbia, MO 65201
Phone: 573-442-0418
Web site: www.offa.org

Pet Industry Joint Advisory Council
1220 19th Street, NW Suite 400
Washington, DC 20036
Phone: 202-452-1525
E-mail: info@pijac.org
Web site: www.pijac.org

Pet Loss Support Hotline
College of Veterinary Medicine
Cornell University
Ithaca, NY 14853-6401
Phone: 607-253-3932
Web site: www.vet.cornell.edu/
public/petloss

Pet Sitters International (PSI)
201 East King Street
King, NC 27021-9161
Phone: 336-983-9222
Fax: 336-983-9222
E-mail: info@petsit.com
Web site: www.petsit.com

Therapy Dogs International, Inc.
88 Bartley Road
Flanders, NJ 07836
Phone: 973-252-9800
Web site: www.tdi-dog.org

UK National Pet Register
74 North Albert Street, Dept 2
Fleetwood, Lancasterhire, FY7 6BJ
United Kingdom
Web site: www.nationalpetregister.org

**United States Dog Agility
Association, Inc. (USDAA)**
P.O. Box 850955
Richardson, TX 75085-0955
Phone: 972-487-2200
Fax: 972-272-4404
Web site: www.usdaa.com

Veterinary Medical Databases
1717 Philo Rd.
Urbana, IL 61803-3007
Phone: 217-693-4800
E-mail: cerf@vmdb.org
Web site: www.vmdb.org

**World Canine Freestyle
Organization (WCFO)**
PO Box 350122
Brooklyn, NY 11235-2525
Phone: 718-332-8336
E-mail: wcfodogs@aol.com
Web site: www.worldcaninefreestyle.org

Further Reading

Everest, Elaine. *Showing Your Dog: A Beginner's Guide*. Begbroke, Oxford, UK: How To Books LTD, 2009.

Gewirtz, Elaine. *Fetch This Book! Train Your Dog to Do Almost Anything*. Pittsburgh: Eldorado Ink, 2010.

Hustace Walker, Joan. *Cocker Spaniels* (Barron's Dog Bibles). Hauppauge, N.Y.: Barron's Educational Series, 2010.

Moffit, Ella B. *Cocker Spaniel: Companion, Shooting Dog, and Show Dog*. Whitefish, Mont.: Kessinger Publishing, 2009.

Morrison, Paul. *Hunting with Spaniels: Training Your Flushing Dog*. Freehold, N.J.: Kennel Club Books, 2009.

Palika, Liz. *Cocker Spaniel*. Hoboken, N.J.: John Wiley and Sons, 2009.

Rice, Dan. *The Complete Book of Dog Breeding*. Hauppauge, N.Y.: Barron's Educational Series, 2008.

Sucher, Jamie. *Cocker Spaniels* (Complete Pet Owner's Manual). Hauppauge, N.Y.: Barron's Educational Series, 2009.

Young, Peter. *Groom Your Dog Like a Professional*. Neptune, N.J.: TFH Publications, 2009.

Internet Resources

www.akc.org/breeds/cocker_spaniel

This page contains the American Kennel Club's description of the Cocker Spaniel breed standard.

www.asc-cockerspaniel.org

The official Web site of the American Spaniel Club provides breed information, a health database, health registry, award listings, a calendar of events, educational materials, and much more.

www.aspca.org

The ASPCA Web site provides expert advice on pet care, animal behavior, poison control, and disaster preparedness.

www.ecsca.org

The official Web site of the English Cocker Spaniel Club of America Inc. provides breed information, breeder referrals, educational materials, event overviews, and other helpful resources.

www.hsus.org

The official Web site of the Humane Society of the United States offers valuable information about pet adoption and pet issues.

www.thekennelclub.org.uk/item/113

This page contains a description of the breed standard for Cocker Spaniels as established by The Kennel Club of the United Kingdom.

Index

Numbers in **bold italics** refer to captions.

Contributors

KAREN SCHWEITZER is a professional writer and dog lover from Michigan. She has written several books for children as well as three other books for the OUR BEST FRIENDS series. Other publishing credits include numerous articles for major magazines, newspapers, and Web sites. Pet care, particularly care for dogs, has always been one of her favorite writing topics. You can learn more about Karen at www.karen-schweitzer.com.

Senior Consulting Editor **GARY KORSGAARD, DVM,** has had a long and distinguished career in veterinary medicine. After graduating from The Ohio State University's College of Veterinary Medicine in 1963, he spent two years as a captain in the Veterinary Corps of the U.S. Army. During that time he attended the Walter Reed Army Institute of Research and became Chief of the Veterinary Division for the Sixth Army Medical Laboratory at the Presidio, San Francisco.

In 1968 Dr. Korsgaard founded the Monte Vista Veterinary Hospital in Concord, California, where he practiced for 32 years as a small animal veterinarian. He is a past president of the Contra Costa Veterinary Association, and was one of the founding members of the Contra Costa Veterinary Emergency Clinic, serving as president and board member of that hospital for nearly 30 years.

Dr. Korsgaard retired in 2000. He enjoys golf, hiking, international travel, and spending time with his wife Susan and their three children and four grandchildren.